TIMELINE OF WAR

TIMELINE OF WAR

R.A. Nicholls

DEDICATION
FOR SKM (#1), KKHD (=2), RAS (X3), CJB (NOW 4) & ALL THE PBI (RIP)

This 2008 edition published by Barnes & Noble, Inc.,
by arrangement with Canary Press.

Barnes & Noble, Inc.
122 Fifth Avenue
New York, NY 10011

ISBN: 978-1-4351-0869-1

Printed and bound in China

10 9 8 7 6 5 4 3 2 1

COVER & INTERNAL DESIGN
Anthony Prudente on behalf of Omnipress Limited

Contents

Introduction

'The most persistent sound which reverberates through men's history is the beating of war drums.'
Arthur Koestler, Janus: A Summing Up

War is most often defined as an open, armed and long-standing conflict that takes place between nations, states or groups of people. It is also possible to declare war against an ideology, an attitude, an object or a group of objects. Governments do this often, declaring (with help from the media) a 'War on Knives', a 'War on Drugs', a 'War against Terror', or whatever else happens to be concerning the public at that particular time.

For a long period, it was generally supposed that war is a construct of man, and that we humans were the only species who engage in it. Interestingly, this is not so. Closer observation of the animal kingdom has discovered wars between ant colonies and chimpanzee tribes. This fact has inspired many philosophers to suggest that war is therefore a state of nature, that it is a part of man's natural instinct that he should feel driven to conquer, to terrorize and, ultimately, to murder his fellow man.

It is certainly true that humans have an instinctive fight or flight response mechanism (as first described by Walter Cannon in 1915), which is built into our bodies. When we are faced with an acutely stressful situation, one that physically threatens our being, the human brain automatically readies the body for one of two reactions. Either we retreat (run away), or stay and fight to defend ourselves. Humans share this fight or flight response with all other intelligent members of the animal kingdom, but, importantly, we have also been granted the gift of reason. It is our ability to reason which – in theory at least – enables us to decipher a real threat from a supposed one, as well as to make moral and practical decisions concerning the possible outcomes of fight as opposed to flight. In humans with active and healthy cognitive function, the automatic fight or flight response system never fails. Sadly, our capacity for reason varies dramatically from person to person, and can fail at any time, even if you happen to be the most powerful man in the world.

Of course, over the years, wars between human beings have had a much more devastating effect on the animal world than any chimpanzee or ant war. This is because as well as our (heinously flawed) capacity for reason, we also possess an innate ability to use and develop tools. The tools of war are some of the most highly developed and efficient ever conceived by human beings, and as a species we seem to take pleasure in thinking up new, interesting and technologically advanced ways to kill people. Animals get caught in the crossfire – their blood shed and their habitats destroyed.

It was the American politician, Charles Sumner, who said, 'Give me the money that has been spent in war and I will clothe every man, woman, and child in an attire of which kings and queens will be proud. I will build a schoolhouse in every valley over the whole earth. I will crown every hillside with a place of worship consecrated to peace.' Beautiful and profound words indeed, but the chances are that wherever in the world Sumner chose to build these churches, somebody somewhere would become upset, either concerning whose land they were built on, or which particular God (or Gods) were worshipped there, and the entire bloody process would begin all over again.

It would be accurate to say that religion plays a central part in many wars, mainly, though not exclusively, because like race, or class, faith offers a point of difference between people. We humans have fought under the banner of one religion or another since the very beginning of civilization, and this simple fact has encouraged many to believe that religion itself is at fault, rather than the people who manipulate religious doctrine in order to gain, or to maintain, power through violence. In exactly the same way, emotive buzzwords, such as 'liberty', 'democracy' or 'independence', can be used to mask a cynical bid for power over land or resources. That does not mean that there is anything wrong with freedom, or democracy, only with the people who use it to kill.

It is under these fake banners that the real evils of war are perpetrated, and the romantic myth that it is somehow noble to die for your country, in the practice of killing others who are under the exact same illusion, perpetuated. Wilfred Owen, a Welsh infantry officer (who won a posthumous military cross exactly three weeks before The Great War ended, in 1918) spoke most effectively for the doomed youth of Flanders – for it is ordinary people, often young, disenfranchised people, who are the worst hit victims of any conflict:

If in some smothering dreams you too could pace
Behind the wagon that we flung him in,
And watch the white eyes writhing in his face,
His hanging face, like a devil's sick of sin;
If you could hear, at every jolt, the blood
Come gargling from the froth-corrupted lungs,
Obscene as cancer, bitter as the cud
Of vile incurable sores on innocent tongues,
My friend, you would not tell with such high zest
To children ardent for some desperate glory,
The old Lie: *Dulce et decorum est*
Pro patria mori.

This book does not set out to lay blame with any party, only to document the evolution of warfare, from its very beginnings to the present day. This book leaves the reader to come to his or her own conclusions about the justness of any of these conflicts. We have chosen to begin at the year 8000BCE, because this is the point at which we have evidence that the first weapons were in use.

EARLY WARFARE

8000BCE–37BCE

8000BCE

Sharpened stone heads are used for axes, spears and arrows. Wood is used for clubs, axe handles and spear shafts. Spears are generally shorter than the warrior and used with one hand. Sling use is limited by the great deal of training needed to use it effectively. However, slings did outrange all other missile weapons, even bows, throughout the 4th century BCE.

7000BCE

Walls in Jericho are built to protect the settlement from human intruders, as well as predators, like Asiatic lions around the Dead Sea (Northern Trans-Jordan). By 6000BCE, the entire city is walled against animals: Jericho appears to have been at war with its neighbours. Successive archaeological excavations, since 1907, indicate that the walls were destroyed many times. But who was the enemy? And what was their quarrel? These questions may set a working year zero for war chronology, about eight millennia ago, when what we may feel we know about human endeavour and conflict begins to be recorded along the riverbanks of the Tigris and Euphrates, and along the Nile, where the amazing Egyptians establish a 'calendar year' based on a solar cycle 360 days long, divided by 12 lunar cycles of 30 days each.

6000BCE

Dry farming is developed in Mesopotamian hills.

6000 – 4000BCE

Tigris–Euphrates plains are colonized.

6000 – 3000BCE

Farming communities spread from south-east to north-west Europe.

Archaeological evidence of the Palaeolithic periods shows pottery production along the southern coast of the Mediterranean Sea. More sophisticated ceramics are produced throughout Babylon and around the Black Sea, suggesting that larger kilns and medium-temperature furnaces are widespread.

By 5000BCE, city-states exist in Mesopotamia. Carbon dating suggests that defensive walls are part of most human settlements, alongside rivers and lakes that act as moats. Who or what they were defending themselves from may never be known: wild animals of course, or flooding – but both the earliest chroniclers and the early masons and builders of humanity were involved in taking threats seriously. They fortified their homes and organized themselves into large collectives, in order to defend themselves.

By 4000BCE, furnaces are working at much higher temperatures, both in Egypt and in Sumeria. Gold and silver are smelted, largely for decorative purposes, but copper alloys are also developing. Metal blades and prongs, shaped into ploughshares, knives and rakes may be seen as the first industrial production of weaponry.

In what we now know as the Middle East, maces – rocks shaped for the hand – are made. Handles are added to increase the velocity and force of the blow. They were difficult to attach to rocks, and the few well-made maces were used only by elite warriors – usually employed and equipped by rich traders, often to protect goods in transit, usually by water or camel caravan.

By 3800BCE, Cretan ships are carrying, trading and bullying using maces and metal weapons around the eastern Mediterranean, creating the first recorded trade wars.

3760BCE

When some semblance of sequence begins to be brought, by Jewish scholars, to the study and recording of human events, there are dynastic conflicts in both Upper and Lower Egypt. The first metal tools commonly used in agriculture (rakes, digging blades and ploughs) are used as weapons by slave and peasant 'infantry' – the first mass usage of expendable foot soldiers.

3500BCE

The world's first ruling war hero emerges from the Nile conflicts: King Menes the Fighter is victorious and establishes ruling dynasties that will last for 700 years. Menes also becomes the first major arms importer by acquiring bronze weapons from Bohemia, where the smelting industry is already using the first type of blast furnace.

Blacksmiths become the most important craftsmen in history; they are rivalled only by masons in terms of prestige. Possibly the first organized form of mock war (team sports) takes place.

Sumerian civilization has developed in the south-east of the Tigris–Euphrates river area. Akkadian civilization has developed in the north-west area. The two engage in continual warfare.

3000BCE

The Bronze Age begins in Greece and China.

Egyptian military civilization has developed, with formal education for weapons tradesmen and some military services.

Composite re-curved bows are being used. The rear, or belly, of the bow is reinforced with horn to increase the bow's resistance to bending. Adding sinew to the front of the bow increases the speed and recoil power. The ends of the bow curve away from the archer when the bow is strung.

3000BCE
Minoan civilization appears in Crete.

In Mesopotamia helmets are made of copper-arsenic bronze, with padded linings.

Gilgamesh, king of Uruk, becomes the first to use iron as a material for making weapons. The Sage Kings in China begin their refined use of bamboo weaponry.

2800BCE

Sumer city-states unite together for the first time.

2700BCE

Palestine is invaded and occupied by Egyptian infantry and cavalry in return for Palestinian attacks on trade caravans in Sinai.

2500BCE

Harrapan civilization in Indian valley has developed.

Middle third millennium BCE

Copper, used for mace heads, is first found in Mesopotamia, then in Syria, Palestine and Egypt.

2500BCE

Sumerians make helmets out of bronze, along with bronze spearheads and axe blades. Blacksmiths begin making maces with ellipsoidal forms, to concentrate force at the point of impact. As helmets become stronger, the mace head becomes sharper and the axe begins to evolve. The difficulty in casting bronze and its limited strength means that axe blades are broad and joined to a handle at three points, with bindings or rivets.

Sumerians begin designing socketed axes, where there is a tubular hole cast in the axe head through which the handle can be placed. Since armour is getting stronger, the axe head needs to be narrower in order to penetrate it; narrow axe heads cannot be made secure simply with bindings and rivets.

Sumerians use chariots, four-wheeled carts drawn by donkeys and wild asses. They lack a pivoting front axle.

Projectile weaponry develops further. Lugazaggisi, king of Uruk, defeats the Lagash Empire, with support from archers.

2350BCE

King Sargon of the Akkadians has bows and arrows mass produced in Mesopotamia. He seizes the entire Semitic Empire, built by Lugazaggisi, and uses the first 'landscape diagrams' to help deploy his troops.

2250BCE

Evidence of maps used in combat during the Hsai dynasties, in China.

2230BCE

Guti people sweep through Babylonia and overthrow the Akkadian Empire.

2130BCE

The Guti are driven out of Mesopotamia.

2000BCE

Sumerian civilization falls. Advanced state societies develop in Crete (Minoan), Greece (Mycenaean) and Turkey.

Hittite tribes become unified around the Bosphorus. From Asia Minor (Turkey), their joint forces cross the Euphrates, plunder Babylon and advance into Syria.

Third and second millennia BCE

Helmets and body armour made of electrum are found in Egypt and Mesopotamia. (Though a weaker metal than others available at the time, the mystical, spiritual and psychological properties of electrum may have been considered just as important as its strength.)

2000–1400BCE

Crete uses ships with keels and ribs.

2000BCE

The Assyrian Empire establishes a colony in Anatolia (Turkey), in order to send metals (especially copper) to Mesopotamia. Hittites build a capital city with 6.4 km (4 miles) of massive defensive walls; Hittites also master iron production and defeat the Babylonians, to the east, and Egyptians, to the south, in battle.

1900BCE

Amorites conquer all of Mesopotamia, including the remnants of the Sumerian civilization.

1850BCE

Babylonian civilization rises to political prominence under the Amorites. It is discovered that hammering can harden copper weapons.

1800BCE

By adopting advanced reconnaissance tactics and attacking with one coherent large force, the formidable warriors of the Hyksos drive the numerically superior Egyptians south, achieving complete control of the Nile delta.

1760BCE

The Greeks begin to use bronze to make armour, swords and spears. Breastplates of bronze, beaten and later moulded to specific shapes, are worn. Greaves – metal plates for the lower leg – are developed soon after breastplates. Bronze is more commonly used than iron, because iron could only be worked in small pieces.

1700BCE

Harrapan civilization falls to outside attacks.

1760–1520BCE

The Chinese Shang dynasty is founded. (above) A 3,200-year-old bronze head from the Shang Dynasty. Jade fittings are utilized in weapons.

1600BCE

Iranian tribes begin using warhorses and light, two-wheeled chariots, in Mesopotamia.

Middle second millennium BCE

Egyptian, Hittite and Palestinian chariots are very light and sophisticated; two or three horses, secured by poles and yokes, draw them.

1575BCE

Egyptian forces, led by Pharaoh Amosis I, use Nile flooding and the first troop-carrying boats to liberate Upper Egypt from the Hyksos. Amosis becomes the first recorded military commander to acknowledge that his victory originated in duplicating the methods of his enemy, especially the Hyksos' use of reconnaissance units and combat training in small units.

1500BCE

Armour of overlapping scales of bronze, laced together or sewn onto a backing of padded fabric, is used in Mesopotamia, Syria and Egypt. Egyptians are still using bindings and rivets for their axes.

The axe has developed into the sickle sword, a bronze sword with a curved concave blade and a straight, thick handle.

1450BCE

The Mycenaeans of mainland Greece take control of Crete.

1400BCE

The Phoenicians develop ships with two banks of rowers on both sides, and rams.

Cleaning impurities from smelted iron produces vastly stronger metals in Syria. Improved weaponry spreads to Egypt and Greece.

1350BCE

Pharaoh Amenhotep IV fundamentally reinvents his army's command structure and equips the infantry with new blades. His attempts to absorb the power of the priesthood into paramilitary structures, however, are resisted.

1299BCE

The Battle of Kadesh occurs between Egypt and the Hittites, over control of Syria, but the result is indecisive.

1250BCE

Moses leads the Israelites into Canaan, away from captivity in Egypt.

c.1250 BCE

Mycenaean raiders, under Agamemnon, sack the city of Troy.

1200BCE

The Iron Age begins. Iron weapons spread among the mass of people and help to trigger widespread migrations. Effective long-bladed swords are developed once iron can be hammered at tensile strength.

Trojan wars produce new approaches to siege conflicts.

Towards the end of the second millennium BCE

Horses are bred with the strength and stamina to carry men. Chariot use has declined greatly.

1193BCE

The destruction of Troy: miners and sappers undermine the walls, and the first large-scale *ruse de guerre* proves decisive when soldiers are infiltrated into the city inside a large wooden horse.

1100BCE

Mycenaean and Minoan civilizations are destroyed by invading Dorians – a primitive people from northern/north-western Greece, who introduce the iron slashing-sword to warfare in the region. They spread throughout Greece and Anatolia.

1090BCE

Civil war in Egypt during the reign of Rameses XI.

1027BCE

The Chou dynasty replaces the Shang dynasty in China. Noble rulers owe their land to the king and give him military service in return.

c.1000BCE

The craft of iron making has become widely spread across Anatolia and Asia Minor (Turkey). Athens begins to organize reoccupation of the Ionian coasts and islands. (Athens is the first centre of Iron Age culture in Greece.) Aryan peoples conquer the Indus Valley area.

1000BCE

Perhaps the first war memorial to emphasize mourning rather than vainglory is sculpted at Deir-el-Bahri, Egypt. It depicts a wounded Syrian soldier, possibly a mercenary, armed with iron weapons, accompanied by his Egyptian wife and son.

The Philistines crush Saul, first king of Israel, in battle.

The Jewish kingdom arises under King David, following the decline of Egyptian power. David unites Judah and Israel (1000–960BCE), with Jerusalem as the capital: he returns the Ark of Covenant and Decalogue to the city and brings water supply through reinforced subterranean tunnels. Jerusalem is therefore established as a fortified city capable of withstanding siege warfare.

Attica is united under the rule of Athenian kings, whose soldiers use hoplite spears 3 m (9.8 ft) long to introduce full democracy.

960BCE
Solomon succeeds David – peace and civilization in Yahweh's Temple.

933BCE Solomon dies. His kingdom is divided between Rehoboam I, as king of Judah, and Jeroboam I, as king of Israel. Neither king can effectively resist the forces of Sheshonk I of Egypt, who cross the Sinai Desert over a series of nights to seize and pillage Jerusalem (possibly the first movement/deployment of major field forces solely at night).

900BCE Adanirari II of Assyria makes a tactical 'peace' with Babylon. He uses the truce to improve his army's stamina and standards of weapons training. The equally devious and militarily aware Assurnasirpal II succeeds him.

880BCE The Assyrian Empire controls the trade routes between the Mesopotamian world and the Mediterranean world from about 890BCE. Assyrians maintain a very centralized and brutal government. They engage in mass murder, deportation and enslavement. Assurnasirpal (883–859) utilizes a professional and internationally recruited army.

850BCE Hellenistic epics: *Iliad* and *Odyssey*, by Homer.

813BCE Carthage is founded as a trading centre with Tyre. Hunting chariots are imported from Kalach; team competitions develop as a form of blood sport combined with military training, leading to the cult/legend of Nimrod the Hunter.

800BCE The noble warrior caste of China assumes responsibility for organizing the government and conducting the worship of its ancestors according to traditional rites.

Eighth century BCE

Tyre falls to the Assyrians and Carthage becomes the leader of the western Phoenicians.

790BCE Civil war in David's kingdoms. Amaziah, king of Judah, is defeated by Israel and later killed by Judaean rebels who oppose his rule.

785BCE Homer describes advanced battlefield surgery.

780BCE 6 September: first authenticated date in Chinese history – solar eclipse.

776BCE The first recorded Olympic games are held in Olympia, largely in celebration of battlefield skills: horse and chariot racing, wrestling, boxing, javelin, discus, running and pentathlon.

770BCE Transport developments – the Etruscans introduce horse-drawn chariots to Italy. Spoked wheels and horseshoes are used by the Halstatt culture.

760BCE Spartans colonize Taranto in southern Italy. Celts move into England.

750BCE The first Messenian war: Sparta gains hegemony in Greece.

"The walls of Sparta were its young men, and its borders the points of their spears"

King Agesileos

720BCE Romulus, first king of Rome, divides a year into 10 months, about 5,000 years after Egyptian solar observations showed there to be 12 lunar rotations annually. (Julius and Augustus Caesar eventually add their names to the Roman calendar to make it work.)

700BCE Achaemenids begin ruling Persia.

680–669BCE
Assyrians conquer Egypt.

Seventh century BCE
There is much conflict in the Huang-ho Valley of China, followed by a conquest of southern areas, as Mongolian horsemen migrate, developing cavalry tactics of speed and brutality, which will lead to the conquests of Attila the Hun.

665BCE King Sennacherib of Nineveh is one of the first tyrants to use his army against his own people.

660BCE Assyrians destroy the city of Babylon. Army engineers divert the Euphrates to cover the site of the city.

650BCE Second Messenian war – Spartan rule is challenged in Greece.

640BCE Judah submits to the Assyrians, whose army moves on to Egypt and destroys both Memphis and Thebes.

630BCE Scythian raiders wage pillage-wars in Palestine and Syria.

625BCE Nabopolassar, a Chaldean general, seizes the Babylonian throne and declares independence from Assyria.

620BCE Mayan civil wars in Mexico are resolved with few casualties. Civilization and culture are established, in peace, for nearly two millennia.

Phoenicians settle in Corsica.

612–609BCE
Medes of Persia and Chaldeans overthrow Assyrians and destroy their capital – Nineveh.

600BCE Iron begins to replace bronze in China.

587BCE Nebuchadnezzar destroys Jerusalem, and Jewish communities are dispersed.

550BCE Cyrus I rebels against the Medes and captures their capital in Ecbatana. Over time, he extends his rule to the Jaxartes and Lydia, where he extracts tribute from the Greeks on the Ionian and Aegean coasts.

540BCE Etruscans and Carthaginians unite at the battle of Alalia.

539BCE The Persians, under Cyrus the Great, capture Babylonia.

Darius I further extends the Achaemenid Empire. His empire is divided into satrapies. It is a complex bureaucracy, with a standing army and a large labour force, which he uses to build cities, roads, temples, vast irrigation networks and palaces. Zoroastrianism is the religion of the state, but other religions are tolerated.

505BCE The Etruscans defeat the Romans, despite a famous rearguard action by Horatius Cocles, who held a Tiber Bridge against the army of Lars Porsena.

500BCE Civilization centred on the Middle East and Anatolia at one end (Persians), and the Mediterranean (settled by colonists from the Levant-land at the eastern end of the Mediterranean, and the Aegean) or Greek world at the other end.

499–494BCE
Persia brutally suppresses the revolts of Ionian cities.

490–449BCE
Greco-Persian wars.

490BCE The Persians use war elephants when defeated by Miltiades at Marathon. News of victory was carried the 39 km (24.2 miles) to Athens by a runner, Pheidippides, causing incredulity among representatives of the warrior-nation of Sparta.

481BCE In China, an age of warring states begins. Standing professional armies are being developed by dozens of principalities. Martial poems are written on stone, bamboo and silk, and miraculously preserved.

480BCE Themistocles, Athenian general and archon, creator of the Greek navy, agrees to lead the Athenian squadron (200 of the 324 Hellenic vessels) against the Persians, under the command of the intrepid Spartan, Eurybiades. After King Leonidas is outwitted at the Battle of Thermopylae, Athens is burned, and the Acropolis destroyed by the vast army of Xerxes I – an army that probably numbered over a million marching men. Themistocles understood that the Persians could only be confronted at sea, so he chose to interdict Xerxes' galleys off Salamis as they advanced towards Corinth, seizing control of the Peloponnesian Peninsula. As the battle approached, it took all of Themistocles' energy to convince his timid superior to await the attack of the enemy. In his eagerness to precipitate a collision, he sent a messenger to urge the Persian generals to make an immediate attack, as the Greeks had resolved on retreat. A great victory was won and Themistocles became a national hero.

THE 300 SPARTANS

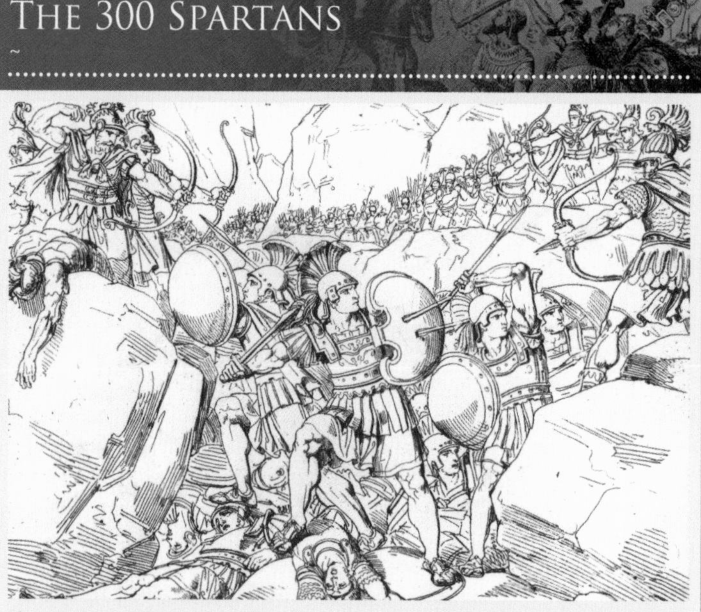

The Spartans have been referred to as one of the most extreme civilizations in history. Their warlike society was focused upon the creation of the ultimate warrior, with an emphasis on discipline and sacrifice by the individual for the good of the group. According to legend, at the battle of Thermopylae in August, 480BCE, 300 Spartan warriors, led by King Leonidas I, sacrificed their lives in order to hold off an enormous Persian Army, led by King Xerxes. The myth states that the 300 Spartans fought, and that 299 of them died in battle. The small Greek force actually consisted of 300 Spartan soldiers, 700 Thespian volunteers, 400 Thebans who had been forced to serve the Greek alliance, and 900 Helots. The Alliance was successful in holding off the Persian army at Thermopylae for a miraculous three days, so that the Athenians could desperately rally their Navy. Unfortunately though Leonidas was betrayed by Ephialtes, who informed Xerxes, another route around the pass. Xerxes led a large portion of his army around the pass in order to attack the Greeks from the rear. Leonidas found out that he had been betrayed and ordered all but a small number of his soldiers (the '300') to stay behind and fight.

> **“ *I am Xerxes, great king, king of kings, the king of all countries which speak all kinds of languages, the king of the entire big far-reaching earth* ”**

King Xerxes, foundation tablet at Persepolis.

480BCE The Carthaginians, led by Hamilcar Barca, are defeated at Himera, Sicily, by Gelo of Syracuse.

479BCE The Greeks, commanded by Spartan general Pausanias, defeat the Persians, at Plataea.

478BCE The walls of Athens are rebuilt and the harbour of Piraeus is fortified.

477BCE 306 Roman Fabii men are slaughtered at Cremera while engaged in a holding/rearguard action against invading Etruscan forces. Hundreds of their armed supporters, their slaves, servants and some of their wives die alongside them.

470BCE Cimon, son of Miltiades, the victor at Marathon, leads concerted campaigns against a diminishing Persian army, which is far from home. Denial of food, water and sleep feature in Cimon's tactics.

466BCE Cimon destroys the Persian army at Eurymedon as their fleet attempts to resupply and reinforce troops on the beach. A total of 200 Persian ships are sunk or captured: others evacuate the remnants of Xerxes' army to the island of Cyprus.

465BCE Gelo forms one of the first all-volunteer armies, when democracy is established in Syracuse.

460BCE At a battle in another Salamis, on Cyprus, the Persians finally collapse.

449BCE Artaxerxes recognizes the independence of all the Greek city-states at the Peace of Callias (probably the first intercontinental peace treaty).

448BCE
Aspasia, mistress of Pericles, rules Athenian society: she is one of the first women to become involved in military command.

445BCE A 30-year formal truce is agreed between Athens and Sparta. It is influenced by both Aspasia and later by Pericles' ward (and kinsman), the orphaned Alcibiades – and later still by an eight-year outbreak of plague in Athens, from 430 to 423BCE.

THE BIRTH OF CHEMICAL WARFARE

'Chemical warfare' is to the use of poisons, toxic gases and other chemical substances to kill, injure or incapacitate an enemy. The use of chemical weapons dates back to the Stone Age, when African hunters used the venom from scorpions and poisonous snakes, as well as toxic plants in the making of poison arrows. The hunter simply hit his prey with the poisoned arrow and stalked the animal until it keeled over. The earliest known use of chemical weapons on the battlefield occurred in China during the 4th or 5th century BCE. The writings of the Mohist sect describe the ingenious use of ox-hide bellows, which were fashioned to pump the smoke from burning balls of mustard and other toxic plants into the tunnels being dug by a besieging army. The Athenians and the Spartans were the first westerners to use various chemical weapons, during the Peloponnesian war between Athens and Sparta. The Spartans used a combination of lighted wood dipped in a combination of pitch and sulphur, in the hope that the noxious smoke would irritate and incapacitate their enemy. The Athenians are known to have used plants such as hellebore root to poison water supplies.

440BCE Both Jerusalem and Rhodes are actively fortified. Nehemiah and Ezra raise walls at the Rock/Temple Mount. Hippodamus of Miletus builds the protected northern harbour and walled town at Rhodes.

431BCE Peloponnesian wars occur between Athens and Sparta, despite the '30-year truce'. Intermittent hostilities continue for the next 27 years, initially caused by Spartan suspicions about the ambitions of Pericles.

> **“ *Trees, though they are cut and lopped, grow up again quickly, but if men are destroyed, it is not easy to get them back again* ”**

Pericles

429BCE Pericles dies. He is succeeded by the strange and strained joint rule of Cleon and Nicias.

421BCE ‘The Peace of Nicias’ initiates another armistice, a ‘50-year truce’ (which lasts six years).

420BCE Cleon dies. Alcibiades moves against the ineffectual Nicias and persuades the Athenians to ally themselves with Argos, Elis and Mantinea against Sparta

408BCE Guerrilla warfare against Persian rule by the Medes, who are put down by King Darius.

406BCE Locked in war against Carthage, democracy is destroyed by the tyranny of Dionysus I (aka The Elder), who introduces catapults as weapons, sometimes firing hot shot.

401BCE ‘Retreat of the Ten Thousand’: a Greek mercenary army led by Xenophon, aiding the Persian prince Cyrus, is defeated at Cunaxa. Xenophon, a disciple of Socrates (as was Alcibiades), described in his *Anabasis* how 10,000 survivors marched home across a thousand miles of enemy territory.

400BCE The Carthaginians occupy Malta.

399BCE Dionysus the Elder of Syracuse directs his engineers to construct military engines for the war with Carthage. The *gastrophetes*, a large crossbow, is an early example of mechanical artillery.

396BCE The Carthaginian army in Sicily destroys Messina.

390BCE Gauls from northern Italy, under Brennus, capture Rome, sack it and burn it.

384BCE Accused of royal ambitions after the failed defence of Rome, Manilus Capitolinus is thrown to his death from the Tarpeian Rock.

379BCE Revolt against brutal Spartan rule in Thebes. ‘Massacre of the Spartan tyrants’ by Pelopidas and Epaminondas.

377BCE Walls rise around Rome, 13 years after the Gallic sacking.

371BCE The Battle of Leuctra. Epaminondas leads Theban forces to victory over a full-scale Spartan army. The first military hegemony of the ancient world is broken: until Leuctra, the Spartans were believed to be invincible.

352BCE Philip II becomes king of Macedonia (reigns until 336BCE).

356BCE Alexander of Macedon, son of Philip II, is born. He will succeed his father in 336BCE, at the age of 19, and die in Babylon in 323BCE, aged 33. In-between, he will become Alexander the Great and will come to understand more about war than any other human being before or since.

Alexander I

~

The man who became known as Alexander the Great will forever be remembered as one of the most talented military men of all time. Alexander of Macedonia was born in July 356BCE. His parents were King Phillip II of Macedon and his wife,Olympias. As a youth, Alexander was educated by the famous scholar, Aristotle, who inspired in him a love of literature as well as geography and ethnology. As a result Alexander developed a good working knowledge of foreign countries and cultures, which helped him during his later career as leader of an immense empire. Alexander must have shown genuine talent for court-life, because he was granted extensive access to foreign ambassadors in his father's court, and at that age of 16, he was named as his father's regent while Phillip was away fighting the Persians. At 18, he commanded the left wing of the cavalry at the battle of Chaeronea. The Macedonian army was victorious, with a decisive cavalry charge led by Alexander.

In 336BCE, Alexander's father was assassinated by a guard (some say according to the plans of his then estranged wife, Olympias), and at the age of 20, Alexander inherited the kingdom of Macedonia. The arrival of a 'new kid on the royal block' sparked rebellion in some Greek provinces, where some people saw it as an opportunity to win back their independence from Macedonia. Alexander's first job was to put a stop to these rebellions. In 335BCE, he raised Thebes to the ground – killing most of the population, and enslaving anyone who happened to escape death. Once Alexander had crushed the Greek rebellions in his own kingdom, he pushed east with his armies in order to conquer the Persian Empire, including Palestine, Syria, Afghanistan, Iran and most importantly –Egypt, where he was made pharaoh. He founded 70 cities in the countries he conquered, the most notable being Alexandria in Egypt. Once he and his armies had reached their furthest point – Northern Pakistan – where his armies finally mutinied – Alexander headed back towards home with the intention of merging all of Europe and western Asia into one single country, with one currency and the city of Babylon as it's capital. This proved to be ambitious, even for Alexander. The lack of working communication systems at the time made such a plan impossible. When Alexander died of malaria, in June 323BCE, he was at the height of his power, and still planning further expeditions. Unfortunately there was one crucial expedition he'd failed to make – the expedition into fatherhood. Alexander died without an heir, and, for all his military genius, his empire did not survive him. Even his tomb, in Alexandria, has been lost in time.

355BCE
The Chinese begin building what will become the Great Wall of China, as partial protection against the Huns.

351BCE Demosthenes stirs Athenian misgivings about Macedonian ambition. A politician and lawyer famed for his oratory, Demosthenes opposed a joint attack on the small city-state of Olynthus in 348BCE, and became leader of the party that advocated resistance to the growing power of Philip of Macedon. In his *Philippics*, a series of speeches, he incited the Athenians to war. This policy resulted in the defeat of Chaeronea, 338BCE, and the establishment of Macedonian supremacy. After the death of Alexander, he organized a revolt; when this failed, he took poison to avoid capture by the Macedonians.

343BCE Philip of Macedon supports the Thebans in 'The Sacred War' against the Phocians.

336BCE Theban turncoats assassinate Philip of Macedon at Aegaeby.

335BCE Now king of Macedonia, Alexander destroys Thebes in revenge for the death of his father.

> ***“I send you a kaffis of mustard seed, that you may taste and acknowledge the bitterness of my victory”***

Alexander the Great

333BCE Alexander begins campaigns against the Persian Empire by defeating Darius, at Issus.

332BCE Having established the great port of Alexandria, the Macedonians conquer Tyre and Jerusalem.

331BCE Staggering Darius's huge army at Gaugamela, by the use of assault troops equipped with 6 m- (19.7 ft) long spears, plus lighter infantry using Roman-type stabbing swords and small, strong, oval shields, Alexander consigns the Persian king to insanity – and then assassination shortly afterwards.

330BCE Alexander the Great takes Babylonia, and plans to make it the seat of his empire.

329BCE Macedonians occupy Susa and Persepolis.

BIOLOGICAL WARFARE

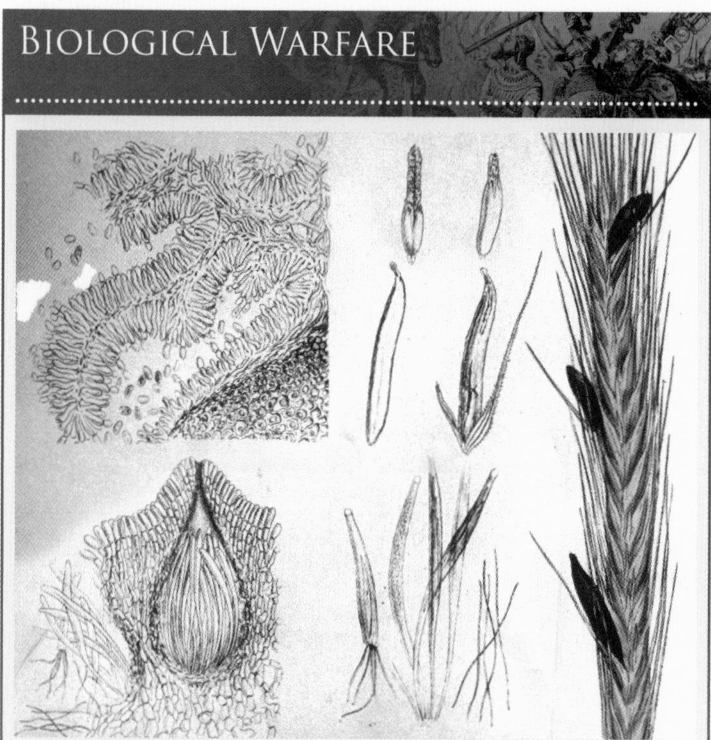

According to the United Nations, 'biological warfare' is the use of any living organism, such as bacterium or any infective component, to cause disease or death in humans, animals or plants. Biological warfare predates the United Nations by thousands of years. In fact such biological weaponry has been used as a crucial tool of war since ancient times because it's usually cheap, easily available and often a naturally occurring by-product of battle. During the 6th century BCE, the Assyrians poisoned their enemies' water supply with ergot (pictured) – a variety of mould that grows on grains and grasses, such as rye. The ingestion of ergot causes a disease called ergotism, or 'St Anthony's fire', which affects circulation and neuro-transmission. The symptoms of ergotism can include severe burning sensations in the limbs, gangrene and loss of limbs, hallucinations, irrational behaviour, convulsions and sometimes death. Armies of various nationalities often dropped diseased corpses into wells in order to poison an enemy population. Vlad Drac (the Impaler) famously poisoned his own people's water supply as he passed through village after village, during his retreat from the Turks – the idea being that the Turks would have no water if they chose to follow him. Vlad Drac cared nothing for his own people, and gladly sacrificed them without thinking. Throughout the centuries, diseases such as plague, leprosy, smallpox, meningitis, hepatitis, anthrax and rabies have all been used by armies to devastate soldier and civilian populations. Although many major countries signed a treaty banning the development and use of biological weapons at the Biological Weapons Convention in 1972, they continue to be used on an unofficial basis all over the world. It is really just the official development, stockpiling and use of biological weapons that has been reduced. The modern threat of bioterrorism is a major concern for governments the world over.

328BCE Alexander the Great marries the Bactrian princess, Roxana.

327BCE Alexander the Great invades India.

327–304BCE
Wars between the Romans and the Samnites of ancient Italy. The Romans are defeated at Caudine Forks in 321BCE but rally to inflict dreadful losses at Lucerian (320BCE), Vadimonian Lake (310BCE) and Perugia (309BCE).

326BCE Alexander the Great has extended his empire to the Indus river, but his health is faltering due to several wounds sustained in battle. He is forced to turn back by a conspiracy of his generals, including Antipater, who had outmanoeuvred and defeated, in 330BCE, the great Spartan general Agis, Polysperchon and Ptolemy Soter.

323BCE Alexander the Great dies of a fever in his moated imperial capital, Babylon, in June. His generals squabble over dividing his conquests.

Ptolemies take Egypt and Seleucids take Syria-Iran (and Palestine in 314BCE). (The Ptolemy dynasty will last nearly 300 years, until the death of Cleopatra in 30BCE.)

322BCE Conflict erupts among the Alexandrine generals.

321BCE Chandragupta Maurya develops an empire in the Ganges and Indus river valley areas by re-conquering northern India from the Macedonians. The Mauryan dynasty is established.

> ***“ A state can indulge in armed invasion only where, by invasion, it can reduce the power of an enemy without in any way reducing its own potential, by making suitable arrangements for protection of its own strategic works ”***

Kautilya, c.320BCE: McNeill and Sedlar (1969)

319BCE Polysperchon restores liberty to Hellenic city-states.

316BCE Cassander, who takes over Macedonia as regent, puts Alexander's mother, Olympias, to death.

311BCE The end of civil wars in what had been Alexander's empire: Lysimachus takes Thrace, and Asia Minor (Turkey) goes to Antigonus.

310BCE Alexander's legacy continues at sea: the Macedonian admiral Nearchus completes his exploration and first charting, ordered by Alexander in 325BCE, of the Persian Gulf, the Euphrates and parts of the Indian Ocean. James Cook will study and use some of Nearchus's charts 2,000 years later.

308BCE Ptolemy Soter establishes the great museum and library at Alexandria, which together become one of the Seven Wonders of the Ancient World.

307BCE The Carthaginians besiege Syracuse.

By the end of the century chainmail appears in Greek art.

CHAIN MAIL

Chain mail is a material made from small metal rings that are linked together to form a mesh. The name comes from two words: 'chain' meaning a series of interlinked metal rings, and the French word 'maille' which is derived from the Latin word 'macula', which means 'mesh of a net'. Chain mail is the oldest form of metal armour. The invention itself probably predates its appearance in Greek art by hundreds of years – the Celtic chieftains are known to have worn it as early as the 4th century BCE. Over time various metals have been used in the making of mail. Bronze was found to be too soft, so it was replaced by iron and later, steel. The material was developed in order to protect the body from sharp-edged weapons, such as swords and spears. It is not known who invented chain mail, but the Roman armies first encountered it whilst fighting the Gauls, and were so impressed by it's performance that they adopted it themselves. Chain mail proved to be so successful, that by the 13th century it was used by soldiers to cover the entire body. Unfortunately, because of its flexibility, mail is unable to guard against bone breaks and fractures. Thankfully though, most medieval doctors were able to set bones, whereas they were less able to cure infection and disease that arose from stab wounds. By the 14th century, metal plate armour began to supplement mail in order to protect against bone-breaks and fractures. Eventually plate armour helped to supplant mail, mainly because the manufacture of chain mail was extremely labour-intensive, and therefore very expensive.

300 to middle third century BCE

Mechanical artillery began to use torsion in addition to tension power, allowing larger and more powerful engines to be built. Torsion catapults could send a javelin 730 m (800 yds). Catapults hurled arrows and darts; ballista (very large catapults) hurled stones.

298 to 290BCE

The third Samnite war: extension of Roman power over Etruscans and the Balkans.

289BCE The Romans are defeated at Atrium by the Senones, a Gaulish tribe.

283BCE The Romans invade and conquer Corsica.

280BCE An energetic but small army lands in Italy, commanded by Pyrrhus, king of Epirus.

THE FIRST PYRRHIC VICTORY
279BCE

The term pyrrhic victory is familiar to most, and has come to mean a victory won at unacceptable cost. The man at the centre of the first pyrrhic victory was Pyrrhus (pictured), king of Epirus - a formidable warrior who seemed to have an unfortunate and uncanny knack for turning victory into defeat. In 279BCE Pyrrhus fought the Romans, under the command of consul Publius Decius Mus, at the battle of Asculum, with help from the Tarentine infantry. John Dryden's translation of Plutarch's Pyrrhus describes the battle:

'They had fought till sunset, both armies were unwillingly separated by the night, Pyrrhus being wounded by a javelin to the arm, and his baggage plundered by the Samnites. That in all there died of Pyrrhus's men and the Romans above fifteen thousand. The armies separated, and, it is said, Pyrrhus replied to one who gave him joy of his victory that one other such would utterly undo him. For he had lost a great part of the forces he brought with him, and almost all of his particular friends and principal commanders; there were no others there to make recruits, and he found the confederates in Italy backward'

279BCE Pyrrhus rallies his troops to drive a Roman force from the field at Aesculum, with the help of Tarentine infantry, nearly all of whom were killed.

278BCE Pyrrhus allows reinforcements from both Tarentum and Epirus to be whittled away by Roman raids. He is unable, in any way, to exploit his victories.

275BCE Despite further support from Argos, Pyrrhus suffers massive defeat at Beneventum, is evacuated with the paltry remains of his forces by the Argive fleet, and is soon killed by rioters in Nauplia protesting his incompetence. Therefore, the term 'Pyrrhic victory' has come to mean 'winning' at such high cost that it is more like a defeat.

274BCE The end of the history of Babylon, as its military caste collapses under post-Alexandrine pressure. Babylonians are re-established in new fortified city known as Seleucia.

272–231BCE

Ashoka expands the Maurya Empire in the Ganges and Indus river valley areas. The empire extends west slightly past the Indus river, east past the Ganges river, north to the Hindu Kush and Himalayan mountains and south deep into the Indian subcontinent. The empire promotes religious tolerance.

267BCE A kind of violent madness seems to overtake Roman society. Calabria is provoked into conflict. Gladiators are forced into public combat to the death. Carthage is mooted as a constant threat to Roman trade and society.

266BCE Calabria is conquered by the Romans.

264–241BCE

The first Punic War between Rome and Carthage. Appius Claudius Pulcher defeats Hiero of Syracuse at Messana, in 264BCE; the Roman fleet defeats the Carthaginians at Ecnomus, in 256BCE; Regulus, attacking Carthage, is captured by Xanthippus the Spartan, in 255BCE; the un-successful siege of Lilybaeum, by the Romans, in 250BCE; Hamilcar Barca takes command of Carthaginian forces in Sicily, in 246BCE; Hamilcar makes peace with Rome – the end of first Punic War, 241BCE.

"I am at war with the living, I have come to terms with the dead"

Hamilcar Barca, Carthaginian general and statesman

264BCE During the first Punic War, the Romans develop boarding ramps for their ships – the first use of landing craft infantry for amphibious assault. Romans use the *gladius*, a 0.6 m- (2 ft-) long stabbing sword. Later the *spatha*, the long slashing sword of the barbarians, becomes popular.

259BCE The Romans encounter advanced Greek medicine, especially for battlefield trauma, through contact with Greek prisoners of war.

250BCE La Tène, Iron-Age people from what is now France, invade southern Britain, encountering only token armed resistance.

246BCE The birth of Hannibal, who will become 'The Great', the most daring and successful of Carthaginian generals. He will eventually carry the Punic Wars to Rome itself.

238BCE Carthage begins its conquest of Spain. Carthaginian mixed with Greek influences lead to the development of a distinct Iberian culture with a quasi-chivalric code of military honour.

221BCE The age of warring states in China ends when the warrior state Ch'in predominates all others. The Great Wall of China is built to keep out northern barbarian horsemen.

219–201BCE

The second Punic War. Hannibal makes an unprecedented crossing of the Alps via the Little St Bernard Pass, invading Italy from the north. He takes Torino and crushes Roman forces under Publius Cornelius Scipio at the Ticinus river, in 218BCE. His war elephants and more mobile cavalry also contribute to another devastating Roman defeat at Lake Trasimene, in 217BCE.

216BCE
The most bloody defeat in Roman history at the Battle of Cannae: Hannibal's army slaughters over 50,000 Romans. Philip V of Macedon is impressed enough to make a formal alliance with Hannibal.

212BCE Romans attempt to distract Carthaginian attention to Sicily: under Marcellus, they seize and burn Syracuse. During the fires that follow, the Greek mathematician Archimedes is killed.

211BCE Carthaginians reach the walls of Rome. Hannibal is forced, however, to split his forces when a force of *hastati* – Roman spearmen – defeats his brother, Hasdrubal, at a ford on the Metaurus river. Hasdrubal's depleted force retreats north towards the sea at Rimini: Hannibal goes south.

209BCE Shih Huang Ti, emperor of China, dies, and rebellion begins.

207BCE The Han dynasty supplants the Ch'in in China, and adopts the principles of Confucius. China is united by language and a legalistic basis of government.

202BCE General Scipio Africanus decisively defeats Hannibal's exhausted army at Zama, effectively ending the second Punic War.

197BCE Wreaking revenge on Hannibal's allies, a huge Roman expeditionary force demolishes Philip V's Macedonian army at Cynoscephelae.

195BCE Hannibal flees to Syria and is given sanctuary by King Antiochus III.

192BCE Hannibal lands, with Syrian forces, in Greece.

191BCE A decisive battle is fought at Thermopylae: Romans dismember Antiochus's forces and pursue them to Magnesia, where the Syrians surrender in 190BCE.

189BCE Rhodian galleys off the Eurymedon river defeat Hannibal, having rejoined the Carthaginian fleet.

185BCE The Shunga dynasty displaces Mauryan rule in India.

182BCE
Hannibal commits suicide in Libyssa in order to deny Roman demands for his extradition.

172BCE Rome and Macedon are at war. A clever cavalry tactician, King Perseus inflicts initial defeats on Roman forces.

168BCE Roman legions regroup at Pydna: Perseus is heavily defeated. A Roman governor controls Macedon. Thousands of Macedonians are sold, cheaply, as 'war reparations' to Roman citizens; men, older women and children cost as little as a day's wage. Nubile young women are considered exotic breeding stock, and cost up to 20 times the price of other Macedonian slaves. So begins the era of Roman domination of the known world.

168–167BCE
The persecution of Jews around Jerusalem, by Antiochus IV. The desecration of the Temple provokes Maccabean revolt.

165BCE Jewish victory. Judas Maccabaeus rededicates the Temple after expelling Syrians.

149BCE (until 146BCE)
Third (and final) Punic War. Roman supremacy is total, and revenge is terrible.

147BCE Corinth is destroyed by the Romans: half of its people burn to death. Carthage is razed and levelled. Of over 500,000 inhabitants, less than 50,000 are left alive. They are all sold into slavery. All of Greece comes under Roman control.

146BCE Roman legions reign supreme throughout seven imperial provinces: Corsica/Sardinia, Transalpina, Gallia, Macedonia, Sicily; plus 'the two Spains' on the Iberian Peninsula and 'Africa' (the southern Mediterranean rim – modern Tunisia through to Libya).

133BCE Asia Minor (Turkey) seized as Rome's eighth province: Roman military superiority absorbs minor resistance with scarcely a flinch.

123BCE Carthage is re-established as the legionary headquarters of Africa province – rebuilding commences.

115BCE The beginning of the empire that will become China. Warriors of the Ch'in return from the north-west, cross the Lop Nor Desert, and occupy the Tarim Basin.

112BCE Analogously, local rulers in North Africa, especially King Jugurtha of Numidia, resist Roman rule. Marius and Sulla crush the Numidians by 105BCE.

First century BCE
Romans develop the *pilum*, a 1.5 m- (5 ft-) long weapon, with one third of it being a spearhead. It has a short range, but the head is made of soft iron and bends back when hitting an object. This prevents it from being thrown back and helps it to hook into an enemy's shield.

90BCE Civil war in Rome: Marius is driven out by Sulla.

71BCE
The revolt of slaves and gladiators, led by Spartacus. The rebel army uses Spartan flame-weapons successfully, characterized as '*Edepol, magnae pilae ignis*', sometimes venially translated as 'Astounding, great balls of fire'. Legions, led by consuls Pompey and Crassus, crush the revolt with maximum cruelty, inflicting thousands of rapes, mutilations and crucifixions.

68BCE The Romans colonize Crete.

63BCE Pompey's legions conquer Palestine and absorb it into the ninth Roman province of Syria, overthrowing the Seleucid Empire established after the death of Alexander in nearby Babylon.

61BCE Gaius Julius Caesar wins his first victory as a general against rebels in Iberia.

60BCE Gaius Julius Caesar returns to Rome, is elected consul, and forms 'the First Triumvirate' with Crassus and Pompey. He advocates extension of Roman colonies in Switzerland, France and Britain.

"If you must break the law, do it to seize power: in all other cases observe it"

Julius Caesar

58–50BCE

Caesar emerges as the most effective leader of mobile military forces since Alexander the Great.

55BCE Caesar conquers Northern Gaul; he also dispatches a punitive expedition to Britain, deploying new Roman warships with catapults, to subdue resistance on landing-grounds.

54BCE What is now southern England becomes part of the Roman Empire. Cassivellaunus, the most powerful Belgic tribal leader, agrees to pay tribute to Rome.

53BCE
Crassus (pictured) is defeated and killed by Parthians at the Battle of Carrhae. Rivalry becomes deadly between Caesar and Pompey for control of Rome.

49BCE '*Alea iacta est*' – 'the die is cast' – when Caesar crosses the Rubicon river (probably the present day Fiumicino, flowing near Rimini, in the same area where, on the Metauro, Hasdrubal of Carthage lost what was to prove the turning point of all the Punic Wars). When Caesar led his army across the traditional boundary between Italy proper and Cisalpine Gaul, he effectively declared war on the Roman republic and brought into metaphor forever the phrasal use of 'to cross the Rubicon', to mean the taking of any irrevocable step.

48BCE Battle of Pharsalia: Caesar outflanks and defeats Pompey.

47BCE Pompey is murdered in Egypt on the orders of Queen Cleopatra VII.

44BCE Conspirators, led by Marcus Brutus and Cassius Longinus, murder Julius Caesar, dictator of Rome.

42BCE The Battle of Philippi. Brutus and Cassius commit suicide after their larger army is defeated by legions led by 'the Second Triumvirate', comprising General Marcus Antonius, Marcus Aemilius Lepidus for the senate, and the Julian heir, Octavius, now known as Gaius Julius Caesar Octavianus. The struggle for Roman power is again reduced to two rivals when the feeble Lepidus is discarded. Mark Antony allies himself with Cleopatra, the last queen of Egypt, and the decisive combat takes place at sea, between the war galleys of the Roman and Egyptian fleets.

> “ ***I will not be triumphed over*** ”

Queen Cleopatra of Egypt

40BCE Roman ships are designed with larger catapults and towers.

37BCE Roman ships are strengthened with beams around the waterline. This is the first recorded use of belted armour.

THE ROMAN EMPIRE

31BCE–476CE

31BCE The Battle of Actium. Octavian's superior ships defeat the fleet loyal to Cleopatra and Mark Antony, who both kill themselves following Octavian's victory. Egypt becomes a Roman province.

30BCE Octavian takes the name Augustus after the overthrow of the Ptolemies. He reigns as virtual, and then actual, emperor for 44 years.

9BCE Roman legions, led by Drusus and Tiberius, push into Germania and extend the boundaries of the empire to the River Elbe.

6BCE As the virtual calendar turns, Judaea is annexed by Rome.

CE

9 On a grey northern European island, whose people would prove the most belligerent in history, Cymbeline, king of the Catuvellauni, is recognized by imperial Rome as *'Rex Brittonum'*.

14 Emperor Augustus dies, succeeded by Tiberius who, with Germanicus, had exacted revenge for the defeat of Varus in two punitive marches into the heart of Germany (year 10).

22 Han dynasty suppresses final pockets of resistance. It rules China for 200 years.

26 Tiberius retires to Capri. Rome is ruled then terrorized by Sejanus, prefect of the praetorian guard, an elite force soon made ambitious by its wielding of power.

37 Tiberius dies 'of excess and superstition' (Tacitus). He is succeeded by Caligula, or Gaius Caesar Augustus Germanicus.

Caligula

Caligula was the son of Germanicus Caesar and Agrippina the Elder. His real name was Gaius Caesar Augustus Germanicus, but he was brought up and educated in legionary camps and nicknamed 'Caligula' or 'little boot' by the infantry, after 'caligae' (meaning boot or sandal), because he chose to wear the common soldiers' footwear at all times. Following the death of Tiberius, Caligula came to power with the overwhelming support of the army, but his rapid deterioration corresponds to the Actorian Actonian principle: he achieved absolute power and was absolutely corrupted. Shortly after the army installed him as leader, Caligula fell ill, and many historians believe, with good reason, that this physical illness triggered a mental illness of some kind. Caligula earned a reputation for ruthless and cruel autocracy, he squandered funds left to him by Tiberius, and torture and execution became the order of the day. He had an incestuous relationship with his sister, Drusilla, and promoted his favourite horse, first to the College of Priests, and then to the rank of consul. In a final act of madness, he declared himself a god, and the guard acted. Caligula was hacked to death by dozens of 'anonymous' swordsmen, who then proclaimed Tiberius's scholarly and reclusive nephew – Claudius – emperor.

43 The Romans invade Britain. Resistance from Caractacus is crushed at Medway. London is founded. Martial, eponymous Roman poet, is born.

50 The use of soap, learned from the Gauls, is made compulsory among northern legions.

54
Claudius is poisoned by his wife, Agrippina, and succeeded by her son Nero (pictured).

58 Ming-Ti becomes emperor of China, moves against military aristocracy and introduces Buddhism.

64 The first persecution of Christians. Martial plutocracies in Rome and elsewhere around the Mediterranean are alarmed by the Christian philosophy of forgiveness.

68 Nero commits suicide; there are eight emperors during the next 29 years. Real authority in Rome remains with individual commanders of legions who can command the loyalty of their soldiers.

70 Jewish revolt against Roman occupation. Jerusalem is pounded and largely destroyed. Flavius Josephus continues his *History of the Jewish War*.

By the year 70, Roman catapults were apparently able to send stones weighing 25 kg (55 lbs), 365 m (400 yds) or further. Roman catapults were referred to as onagers, or wild asses, because their rears jump upwards from the recoil.

98 Under Emperor Trajan (until 116), the Roman Empire reaches its furthest geographical extent and starts to systematically record its military conquests. Trajan's Column is erected in the Forum.

During the first century CE, Romans begin to use the segmented iron torso armour – *lorica segmentata* (plate armour), which helps to defend the wearer against smashing and heavy piercing blows.

117 Emperor Hadrian (until 138). Tacitus first publishes his *Historiae*. The first Sanskrit inscriptions in India record aspects of warfare.

121
Hadrian (pictured) visits Britain, and orders the construction of a fortified wall from Tyne to Solway (Hadrian's wall is completed in 127).

122 Jewish rising under Bar Kokhba. Guerrilla resistance continues for 12 years.

161 Marcus Aurelius becomes emperor.

164 Plague spreads throughout the Roman Empire. Little travel or military activity for 16 years.

180 A Roman expeditionary force in Scotland is defeated. The IX Legion retreats south of Hadrian's Wall.

190 Albinus proclaims himself emperor in Britain, but is killed at the Battle of Lyons.

199 The Bishop of Rome gains a predominant position as pope and recruits his own soldiers.

200 Huns invade Afghanistan.

201 Carthage, under Roman rule, begins to emerge as possibly the world's greatest city.

During the 2nd century, square/rectangular Roman fortresses are used along communication routes.

212 Under Emperor Caracalla, Roman citizenship is granted to every freeborn subject throughout the empire.

220 Civil wars in China. The Han dynasty falls and four centuries of strife and division begin.

221 Goths from eastern Germany invade Asia Minor (Turkey) and the Balkan Peninsula.

225 Civil wars start in India, after the ending of the Andgra dynasty in the Deccan region. Southern India breaks up into a dozen kingdoms, all heavily armed.

235 Emperor Alexander Severus is murdered at a meeting with his top generals.

238 His successor, Maximinus, is similarly assassinated while inspecting his troops.

248 Rome staggers towards, and celebrates, the 1000th anniversary of its founding.

257 Goths start to become Europe's most successful war-machine. They divide into Visigoths, who probe into Macedonia, and Ostrogoths, who march towards the Black Sea. The stretching of the legions continues:

Franks invade Spain.

258 Alemanni, supported by Suevi, conquers most of northern Italy, but is defeated by the Roman army at Milan. In order to stave off the 'northern barbarians', the cohort system, established by Marius and Scipio Africanus, has to be substantially revised.

268 Goths sack Athens, Sparta and Corinth.

During the 3rd century, Roman fortresses are using flanking towers and are built with thicker walls, fewer gates and wider moats.

270 Emperor Aurelian advances to meet the Marcomanni from Bohemia after they cross the Danube.

271 Aurelian is regarded as '*resitutor orbis*', which translates as 'restorer of the world', after he defeats both the Marcomanni and the Allemanni, and rebuilds the walls of Rome.

284 Diocletian becomes emperor and recognizes the reality of Rome's position.

285 The empire is partitioned into west and east. Carausius, commander of Roman fleets in British waters, seizes the opportunity to proclaim himself a third emperor, of an independent Britain.

305 Diocletian abdicates in the eastern empire, as does Maximian in the west. They are succeeded by Constantius Chlorus and Galerius, respectively. Neither commands the respect of their military.

306 Emperor Chlorus dies at York. His son, Constantine, who becomes 'the Great' and reunites the two empires again, under Rome, succeeds him.

325 Constantine ends gladiatorial combats in Rome.

330 On the site of the old Greek colony of Byzantium, Constantine founds a new city to serve as an imperial capital.

During the 4th century, Roman fortress walls begin following the contours of the ground on which they are situated.

331 The seat of the reunited Roman Empire moves from Rome to 'Constantinople' (now modern-day Istanbul). This symbolic move would endure for only nine years: the empire splits again in 340.

350 Fortifications are built in London, particularly against attack from the tidal river.

360 From the north, Picts and Scots cross Hadrian's Wall and attack Roman settlements in northern England. From the east, the Huns pour over the far borders of Europe.

370 'Rome's wisest general', Theodosius, drives Picts and Scots back beyond Hadrian's Wall.

376 Huns invade Russia.

378 Emperor Valens is defeated and killed by the fast horsemen of the Visigoths at Adrianople in Thrace. The Battle of Adrianople traditionally marks the beginning of cavalry development and tactics.

Theodosius I

Falvius Theodosius was Roman Emperor from 379 to 395CE, and has come to be known as Theodosius the Great, because he was the last Roman emperor to maintain control over the whole empire – east and west. He was born in January 347, in Cauca, Hispania (modern-day Coca, in Spain), to Theodosius the Elder –one of Emperor Valentinian I's generals. At the age of 21, Theodosius the younger accompanied his father to Brittania (modern day Britain) in order to help suppress the Great Conspiracy of 368. By 374, Theodosius had been promoted to dux (a kind of military commanding duke) of Mosiae, a Roman province on the lower Danube. However, this position of power did not last long. His father, Theodosius the Elder, was suddenly executed by Valentinian as penance for some long-forgotten misdemeanour, and Theodophius Jr, quite wisely, retired to the relative peace and quiet of Spain.

The death of Emperor Valentinian created chaos in the Roman Empire, and fearing further reproach from Valentinian's successors, Theodosios continued to keep a low profile. That is until Gratian appointed Theodosius co-augustus (co emperor) for the Eastern Roman Empire. Gratian was killed during a rebellion in 383, and Valentinian II (co ruler of the Western Roman Empire) died in 392, making Theodosius sole emperor for the entire Roman Empire. Theodosius promptly appointed his son as Honorius Augustus, and co-ruler for the West, in order to safeguard a legacy for his line. As emperor, Theodosius took control of the Roman struggle against the Goths, and was successful in settling the Visigoths in Moesia, as members of the Roman Empire.

379 Theodosius, first Hammer of the Scots, enhancing his reputation for tactical wisdom, negotiates an end to Visigoth warfare by settling them in the empire as citizens. Their new home is in northern Greece, where Theodosius then forbids the Olympic Games.

392 Theodosius reunites the Roman Empire for the last time, and for just three years, until his death.

395 On the death of Theodosius, Alric, king of the Visigoths, considers his people released from agreements with him. His formidable mounted armies strike into southern Greece, plunder Athens and turn west into the Balkans. No organized Roman resistance meets them: the legions are too slow and too poorly equipped to confront Alric's forces.

401 Alric's growing army crosses into Italy.

410 Alric captures and sacks Rome. He directs his horsemen on to Naples, with the intention of invading Sicily via Messina. Old wounds catch up with him near Cosenza, however, and Alric dies. He is buried in the bed of the Busento river, according to Gothic custom. His campaign has one lasting effect: the Roman legions in Britain are withdrawn for the specific purpose of regaining the Italian mainland.

> ***“ The Romans therefore informed our country that they could not go on being bothered with such troublesome expeditions... Rather, the British should stand alone, get used to arms, fight bravely, and defend with all their powers...their life and liberty ”***
>
> Gildas, *c.*540, 1978 trans

416 There are further successes for the Visigoth cavalry, when they conquer the Vandal kingdom in Spain.

420s The Romans are powerless to prevent vast areas of the empire being occupied by people they regard as barbarians. The Vandals take southern Spain; the Visigoths and the Suevi take northern Spain and Portugal; the Franks settle in Gaul and the Huns in Pannonia; while the Ostrogoths hold Dalmatia. In the areas of southern Britain vacated by the legions, Saxons and Jutes drive away another Scots/Pict invasion – and the Angles come to stay, giving their name to the healthy and fertile soil of Angle-terre.

436 The last Roman troops leave Britain.

443 The last Romans are driven from North Africa by Gaiseric, king of the Vandals, and Alans, who had crossed from Spain via the Straits of Gibraltar and seized Carthage in 439, making it the capital of his new dominions.

455 Gaiseric builds perhaps the first maritime empire, using his fleets to raid and terrorize as far as the Peloponnesus. Rome itself is seized by a Vandal fleet from the Tiber, with terror, pillage and arson lasting for 14 horrendous days. Gaiseric carries off the empress and her two daughters among thousands of other slaves.

457 Britons are defeated by Hengest, at the Battle of Crayford: Kent is abandoned to the Jutes.

457 (also 460 and 468)

Roman fleets attempt repeated rescue missions against Gaiseric: their clumsy attempts to ram the nimble Vandal warships are disastrous. The defeat off Cartagena, in 460, is probably one of the biggest naval failures in known military history.

The last half-dozen western emperors implode in just 11 years: Severus (died 465), Athemius (467), Alybrius (473), Glycerius (474), Julius Nepos (475) and the derisively titled Romulus Augustus (476). The end comes when the Herulian mercenary warrior Odoacer drives Julius Nepos from his throne, captures and executes Orestes of Placentia and makes a puppet of Orestes' son, scoffed at as 'Augustulus'. Odoacer then storms the city of Pavia and proclaims himself 'King of Italy'.

476 The eastern emperor Zeno encourages (and bribes) the Ostrogoth king, Theoderic, to invade Italy and depose Odoacer. The world's greatest empire expires, in Edward Gibbons' words, under the weight of its own 'immoderate greatness'.

Meanwhile, and elsewhere, between 481 and 484 a revolt, led by Vahan Mamikonian, secures religious and political freedom for Armenia.

MIDDLE AGES

489–1492

489 At the head of an army of 25,000 men, Theodoric outmanoeuvres Odoacer on the Isonzo river, pursues his retreating forces and defeats him again near Verona.

491 Saxons capture Pevensey, Sussex.

493 Odoacer surrenders to the Ostrogoths at Ravenna. Theodoris strangles him with his own hands, marries the sister of Frankish king Clovis I, and founds the Ostrogoth kingdom of Italy.

494 Theodoric's kingdom absorbs Malta.

496 Clovis defeats the Alemanni near Strasbourg, with the help of Ostrogoth cavalry trainers.

500 The Marcomanni, a German tribe occupying Bohemia, invade and seize Bavaria. On their departure, the Czechs settle in Bohemia – permanently.

The Langobards (aka Lombards) move north of the Danube and probe aggressively: an expansion described as 'seeking occasions for war'.

Indigenous British forces secure a narrow victory over the Saxons at Mount Badon, Dorset.

During the 6th century, a war saddle with a single girth is introduced. The Avars are using stirrups.

507 Clovis of the Franks annexes the Visigoth kingdom of Toulouse after victory in the Battle of Campus Vogladensis.

511
Death of Clovis. His kingdom is divided among his four quarrelsome sons, with courts at Paris, Orleans, Soissons and Metz.

525 Afro-Arab war: Caleb of Abyssinia conquers the Yemen. It is possible that some of his forces are landed by primitive paddle-wheel boats propelled by mule or bullock-powered whim-drive.

536 Dissolution of the Ostrogoth kingdom. Provence becomes part of the Frankish kingdom.

537 Battle of Camlan: Arthur, king of the Britons, is killed.

539 War between the Byzantine Empire and Persia.

551 The Ostrogoth fleet is scattered by the Byzantine navy and forced to retreat further through Ionian and Aegean seas.

552 Totila, last king of Rome, is killed at the Battle of Taginae, fighting against Narses' Byzantine army.

553 Narses, a eunuch general, annexes Rome and Naples for the Byzantines.

559 An army of Huns are repulsed near Constantinople by Belisarius.

565 The quarrelsome and well-equipped army of the Lombards drive the Byzantines from northern Italy, as far as Ravenna.

567 Leovigild, king of the Visigoths, drives the Byzantines from western Spain.

570 Persians overthrow Abyssinian rule in Yemen, renewing the war with the Byzantines.

577 The English of Wessex defeat an outnumbered Cymraeg army at Deorham.

585 Leovigild completes the Visigoth conquest of Spain.

600 Czechs and Slovaks settle into Bohemia, Yugoslavs into Serbia.

The iron stirrup and curb bit are introduced among western cavalry.

613 Ethelfrit leads Northumbrians to victory over Briton forces near Chester.

614 Persians take both Damascus and Jerusalem.

616 Persians overrun Egypt.

619 Persians cross the Hellespont.

626 Persians and Avars attack Constantinople, and are repelled by forces loyal to Emperor Heraclius.

627 The Persians are beaten decisively by the Byzantines under Heraclius, at Nineveh, in a battle conducted largely on horseback. The Byzantine victory is an ode to the stirrup, unknown to Persian riders.

634 'Holy War'. Prophet Muhammad's adviser, Omar, succeeds Abu Bekr as caliph. Omar then conquers Syria, Persia and Egypt and defeats Heraclius, who has gone on to rout the remaining Persian forces.

635 Damascus becomes the capital of the caliphate, as Muslim Arabs capture Gaza.

637 Jerusalem falls to the Arabs.

638 Persia appeals to China for help against the Muslim invaders.

639 The Arabs attack Armenia.

640 Arabs find the Greek museum, at Alexandria, full of treasures dating back more than 1,000 years and the Roman-organized library containing over 300,000 papyrus scrolls from the first Pharaohs and Abraham. The entire collection is smashed and burned.

641 By also destroying the book-copying industry there, the occupying Arab army ends the Alexandrian School as a vital centre of western culture.

Another Arab army, under Omar, destroys all remaining forces of the Persian Empire. The religion of Zoraster is replaced by Islam. Caliphs rule Persia until 1258.

643 The Arabs consolidate conquests in Syria, Mesopotamia and Egypt; then move on to seize Tripoli.

644 The Chinese invade Korea.

646 A Byzantine fleet recaptures Alexandria.

649 The Saracens capture Cyprus, using amphibious landing tactics learned from the Byzantine fleet.

650 The Khazars conquer the empire of the Bulgars in southern Russia.

652 The Saracens agree with the Nubians that Aswan should be the southern limit of Arab expansion.

655 The Byzantine fleet is outmanoeuvred and decimated by Saracen ships at Lycia.

663 Constans II is the last Byzantine emperor to visit Rome. His requests for military assistance fall on deaf ears.

670s Saracen expansion along the entire coast of North Africa.

674 Saracen hegemony reaches as far as the mouths of the Indus river, beyond modern Karachi.

675 Bulgars, driven from Rossiya by Khazars, settle south of the Danube, on the marshlands, which will develop into modern-day Bulgaria.

676
The Saracens besiege Constantinople. Byzantine defenders use catapults to attack with 'Greek fire', invented by Kallinikos. Originally a mixture of sulphur, rock salt, resin and some oil, it is refined, by 678, as a missile weapon containing petroleum, pitch and saltpetre, which ignites on contact with seawater.

685 The victory of the Picts, at Nechtansmere, ends Northumbrian hopes of control over Scotland.

687 The victory of Pepin the Younger, at Testry, unites the Frankish kingdoms. The Carolingian dynasty (named after Pepin's son, Charlemagne) become hereditary 'Mayors of the Palace', and rule France for 300 years.

693 Saracens inflict a crushing defeat on an army led by Emperor Justinian II at Sebastopolis, Cilicia (Turkey).

694 The Arabs / Saracens overrun Armenia.

697 The Saracens destroy Carthage (again).

700 The Arabs conquer Algiers. Christians and adherents of other non-Islamic religions are almost entirely exterminated.

710 Bulgarian horsemen probe towards Constantinople, retreating to their marsh strongholds as winter bites.

Kashgarians appeal to China to help resist Saracen invasion. The Chinese refuse, just as Persia was refused military help in 638.

711 The Arab / Saracen / Moor General Tarik annihilates the armies of King Roderic at Xeres de la Frontera. All of Spain, except Asturius, becomes a Muslim state.

712 The Saracens occupy Samarkand, and make it a centre of Islamic culture.

715 The Muslim Empire extends from Seville to China, with Damascus as its capital.

717 Leo III seizes the throne of Byzantium from Theodosius III and is immediately besieged in Constantinople.

718 After defending his capital city for 13 months, Leo's small fleet uses new ramming tactics, plus shipboard catapults, with Greek-fire missiles. The Arab fleet in the Sea of Marmara is destroyed.

720 On land, the Saracens remain all-powerful. They settle in Sardinia and Tarik's army crosses the Pyrenees into France, seizing Narbonne. Arab science also reigns supreme: chemistry makes advances well beyond Greek fire, particularly in the laboratories of Abu Masa Dshaffar, who probably invented sulphuric acid, nitric acid, nitrate of silver and aqua regia – a mixture of nitric and hydrochloric acids which dissolves all metals except silver.

720s Peace in China contrasts with war in Europe. Buddhist civilization, headed by Emperor Ming Huang, flowers in music and literature. Ch'ang-an is the largest city in the world (Constantinople is second).

725 While Arabs ravage southern France, Charles Martel's army crosses the Rhine and conquers as far south and east as Bavaria. The old realms of the Alemanni become part of the Frankish Empire.

732 A turning point in European history. Strengthened by German cavalry, Charles Martel defeats Arab armies at Tours and Poitiers, stemming the tide of their westward advance.

735 Martel conquers Burgundy.

739 Pope Gregory III asks Martel for military help against Lombards and Greeks, as well as the Saracens.

741 Martel dies. His son, Pepin the Short, becomes mayor of the Frankish Court.

742 Birth of Pepin's son, Charlemagne.

746 Byzantine Emperor Constantine V invades Syria.

747 Constantine's fleet destroys a larger Arab fleet off Cyprus, further strengthening the impression that the Byzantine Empire is at last on the offensive against Arab / Muslim expansion.

751 In a vast battle at Samarkand, an inexperienced Chinese army is shattered by Arab forces and forced to cede west Asian dominion. Chinese prisoners of war teach the skill of paper manufacture to their captors.

752 Cuthred of Wessex is victorious over Ethelbald, at Burford in the Cotswolds. Constantine's resurgent army invade the Abasid Caliphate of (modern) Turkey and Iraq, again holding ground long enough to liberate many Christians and then to resettle them in the

Balkans, strengthening another Byzantine frontier.

753 Pope Stephen III requests and receives assistance from Pepin, who helps to create the Papal States.

754 Kormisosh of Bulgaria raids into Byzantine territory as far as the Anastasian Wall. In long and successive campaigns relying largely on naval power, Kormisosh, and six further Bulgarian kings, will be deposed by Constantine V and his marines.

756 The enlightened Tang emperor, Ming Huang, loses all influence. Caliph Al-Mansur sends Persian troops to help crush rebellion against the new emperor, Hsüan Tsung, at the price of further Chinese concessions in central Asia.

759 After bitter fighting, the Franks finally regain Narbonne from the occupying Arabs.

763 Al-Mansur moves his capital from Damascus to Baghdad.

Battle of Anchialus: 800 Byzantine ships carry 9,600 cavalry to victory over the Bulgars – the heaviest amphibious lift in military history so far.

765 The Tibetan army invades China.

771 Charles, son of Pepin, becomes sole ruler of the Frankish kingdom upon the death of his brother, Carloman. He will soon become 'Charles the Great' – Charlemagne.

772 Charlemagne subdues Saxony and converts Widukind's 'pagan' army to Christianity. He imposes tithes to support his ever-increasing army – and for the support of the clergy, churches, schools and the poor. Pope Hadrian I begs Charlemagne for help against the Lombards.

773 Charlemagne annexes the Lombard kingdom.

774 Charlemagne confirms the promises of his father, in 753, regarding the cession of territory to the pope, and further enlarges the Papal States, in 781.

775 Tibet subdues Himalayan countries and concludes a lasting boundary agreement with China.

776 The Byzantine cavalry are again victorious over Bulgars, at Lithosoria.

778 Charlemagne's first defeat becomes the theme of *The Song of Roland*. In the high Pyrenees, at Roncesvalles, Basque fighters outmanoeuvre a Frankish army in the snow.

780s Construction of Offa's Dyke, to ward off Cymraeg attacks on Mercia.

782 Charlemagne issues '*Capitulatio de partibus Saxoniae*', a template for future demands relating to unconditional surrender, and executes the 4,500 Saxon hostages the Franks hold at Verdun.

787 First Danish coastal raids leading to the invasion of Britain.

788 Charlemagne deposes Tassilo of Bavaria and annexes most of what was the 'Sudetenland' into the Franks' empire.

790s The beginning of the Viking era in Britain.

793 East Anglia invaded by the Mercian army, under King Offa, who annexes the flatlands eastwards as far as the Nordsee.

798 The Mercians, under Cenwulf, subdue and annex Kent.

799 Charlemagne reaches the Adriatic: his armies take the port of Fiume and destroy it.

800 On Christmas Day, Charlemagne is crowned as first Holy Roman Emperor by Pope Leo III, in Rome, therefore reviving the Roman Empire of the west – as opposed to that of the east: the continuing Byzantine Empire.

CHARLEMAGNE

Charlemagne (Charles the Great) was the first king of the Frankish empire, and the first Christian Roman emperor of the west. He did a lot to characterize medieval Europe and presided over the Carolingian Renaissance. He was born in the late 740s near Liege, in modern-day Belgium. His father was Pepin the Short, the Frankish king. Pepin died in 768, and Charlemagne and his younger brother Carlomann inherited his kingdom. Carlomann died suddenly in 771, and Charlemagne became sole ruler of the Frankish kingdom. Charlemagne spent the early part of his royal career on a mission to expand his kingdom. In 772, the year following his brother's death, Charlemagne invaded Saxony. He was eventually victorious and succeeded in converting the whole region to Christianity. He also expanded his territory southwards – successfully invading northern Italy, which had been under the control of the Lombards. His attempt to conquer Spain, which belonged to the Moors, had to be abandoned, but only because he was needed elsewhere. In the years between 780 and 800, Charlemagne successfully conquered Bohemia and created a safe 'buffer state' to the east of his kingdom by subduing the Avars in the middle Danube basin. In 800, a rebellion against Pope Leo III threatened the papacy, and Charlemagne and his armies stepped-in to suppress it. As thanks for his assistance, Pope Leo crowned Charlemagne emperor of the Romans under the name 'Carolus Augustus', cementing his power over his Italian subjects. Charlemagne's enormous kingdom, which now stretched from the River Ebro in Northern Spain to the River Elbe in Germany, became known as the Carolingian Empire. He made many important changes, including the introduction of standardized weights and measures, as well as customs dues – all of which helped to improve trade links and initiate legal reforms. He encouraged the arts, established libraries, made improvements to relations with the east and worked tirelessly toward creating a united Europe, pre-empting the eventual creation of the European union, and the establishment of the Euro.

800 During the 9th century, large, wheeled, wooden siege towers (called belforys), with a drawbridge, are used against fortifications. Battering rams are used as well. Large ones are mounted on wheels in a covered 'shed'. Also during the 9th century, the crossbow appears.

807 Inevitably, Charlemagne's Roman Empire, the Holy version, of the west, is confronted and opposed by the Byzantine, formerly Roman Empire, the anti-Arab version, of the east.

813 The deathly-ill Charlemagne the Great crowns his son, Louis the Pious, at the Diet of Aix-la-Chapelle, at almost the same moment that Leo V becomes emperor in the east.

815
Egbert of Wessex defeats the Kernow-Britons, in Cornwall.

817 Louis the Pious starts to dismember his father's empire: France is divided among Charlemagne's three grandsons, Lothar, Louis and Pepin.

824 Egbert continues to subdue British part-states with his Frankish-trained horse troops.

825 With the defeat of the Mercian army at Ellendun, Egbert controls and unites most of what is now England.

826 The Saracens conquer and settle Crete, preparing it as a maritime base from which to raid, plunder and seize further vulnerable islands in the Aegean, Ionian and Mediterranean seas.

827 Saracens establish bridgeheads in both Sicily and Sardinia.

828 Egbert of Wessex is recognized as overlord of the 'Seven Kingdoms of the Heptarchy'.

830s Regular Danish raids on England.

837 Wessex mobilizes resistance to Danish raiders.

838 Arabs sack and burn Marseilles and Naples. They establish permanent colonies and bases in the far south of Italy. Brought to battle at Amorion, in Asia Minor (Turkey), they rout the major land forces of the Byzantines.

840 The Danes land, unopposed, in Ireland. They settle and found what will become the cities of Dublin and Limerick.

842 Michael III becomes Byzantine emperor. Turkish mercenary soldiers defect to Arab armies.

844 After a long campaign against the Picts, Kenneth, king of the Scots, becomes sole monarch of the cold lands north of Hadrian's Wall, as Kenneth I MacAlpin.

846 The Arab army sacks Rome and burns the Vatican, while Saracen warships sail north into the Adriatic and destroy the Venetian fleet.

848
Pope Leo IV builds the Leonine Wall around the Vatican hill, to help protect it from future attack.

850 The Tibetan regime succumbs to decadence: after riots in several provinces, centralized authority collapses in most of the territory it rules.

851 The Danish fleet enters the Thames estuary, landing raiders who march on Canterbury and sack and burn the cathedral. As they head back to the coast, they are intercepted and routed by English forces at Oakley, Kent.

858 Vikings reach the Pillars of Hercules: they seize Algeciras, across the bay from the Rock of Gibraltar, and remove or burn everything valuable, before an Arab/Moor force expels them.

859 Norse longboats force passage through the Straits at Gibraltar and achieve almost free range in the Mediterranean. With speed and brutality they strike at ports and harbours as far east as the Dardanelles, possibly linking with land forces from Danzig, via the Crimea and Black Sea.

861 Inland, too, Viking rapine seems unstoppable – they sack Frankish towns, from Paris to Toulouse and Aix-la-Chapelle, and make river-raids, from Worms to Cologne. They also discover Iceland and establish settlements near many of the island's warm springs.

865 Northmen, from Rossiya, attack Constantinople.

Danish raids grow into coastal and riverside bridgeheads in Northumbria; then into farming settlements.

868 Danes establish a new kingdom at York under King Guthfrith. Their 'marine' fighters develop into an occupying garrison.

869 Malta falls to an Arab fleet.

877 After bloody but indecisive fighting, Mercia is partitioned between the English and Danes.

878 King Alfred retakes London from the Danes and forces them to a pitched battle and defeat at Edington. The Danes agree, by the Treaty of Chippenham, to a five-year truce.

King Alfred and the Danes

Alfred (pictured), son of King Ethelwulf, was the fourth of his brothers to inherit the throne of Wessex. He is most famous for spending most of his life in battle against the Danes. Alfred was crowned king of the West Saxons in 871, having helped his brother, Ethelred; fight the Danes at the battle of Ashdown. The Saxons were victorious on that occasion, but they lost subsequent battles and as a result they were forced to pay tribute to the Danes.

As king, Alfred was determined not to surrender. He had a earned a reputation as a formidable warrior, and he used it to rally a militia from Somerset and Wiltshire and drive the Danes out of the south west of England at the battle of Eddington. He achieved a partition in the treaty of Wedmore – which helped to establish a Danish area in England called Danelaw. During the war, Alfred made some clever defensive moves, which ensured that the Danes would not be successful in any subsequent invasions. He strengthened his existing forts and built new ones, he improved his navy – building larger ships to defend against coastal raids and he worked to better relations with Mercia and Wales – lending his support to them by sending troops to fight in their armies. This diplomatic 'back-scratching' also helped to strengthen his position.

In 897, six Viking longships arrived on the south coast of Wessex. They raided and looted the Isle of Wight, and in response Alfred sent nine of his newly constructed longships to intercept the raiders. When Alfred's fleet arrived, three of the Viking's ships were beached, and another three stood guard. Alfred commanded his troops to attack the guard ships, and they captured two of the ships and killed all but five Vikings on the third ship. Alfred's ships ran aground, three landing on one side of the estuary and six on the other. The Viking raiders attacked, but they were out-numbered by Saxons, because Alfred's longships could carry more troops. The Saxons killed 120 Vikings, while the Saxons came away with a loss of 62 men. The Viking's smaller longships meant they were better designed to escape in a hurry, and so they did, but the crews on board were so battered and depleted that only one ship made it home to East Anglia. Two ships came ashore in Sussex, where their crews were captured.

Alfred was an inspirational ruler off the battlefield as well as on it. He was a committed scholar, and most of his emphasis was on education. The reason for this is interesting. Alfred believed the Viking raids were punishment for his people's sins, which he put down to a lack of education. In response, he encouraged learning wherever he could. He offered patronage to Welsh and European scholars, learnt Latin himself and translated some important books so that his people could have greater access to the knowledge of the day. His educational policies can also be seen as sound military strategy, he worked to a principle that still rings true for many today – the more you educate people, the more peace-loving they will become.

879 The Arabs conquer the rest of Sicily and make Palermo its capital.

881 The Spanish build the great citadel of Burgos in Castile ('Land of Castles'), as part of frontier defences against further and expected Arab/Moor attacks.

886 Leo VI, 'the Wise', becomes Byzantine emperor.

890 Alfred the Great of England formally institutes a regular militia and navy, using their officers to extend the crown's power over trials, contracts, fairs, markets, navigation and public order.

895 Alfred's navy defeats the Danish fleet on the Lea river, successfully capturing many of the Norse ships intact.

> ***"Then King Alfred had long ships built to oppose Danish warships. They were almost twice as long as the others. Some had 60 oars, some more. They were both swifter and less flexible and also higher than the others. They were built neither on Frisian nor the Danish pattern"***

The Anglo-Saxon Chronicle, 1961 trans

897 Savage fighting occurs between Bulgars and Saracens near Sofia.

899 The death of Alfred the Great.

900 The new century sees the beginning of the Christian reconquest of Spain, led by Alfonso III of Castile.

901 Viking advances in the art of shipbuilding – vastly stronger keel and rib construction; use of swivel pulleys for sails. Oceanic voyages are becoming common, leading to the projection of Viking power into Vinland (Greenland) and then across the Atlantic into what would ironically be called, half a millennium later, 'New Found Land', at L'Anse-aux-Meadows.

904 Muslim pirates sack Salonika. Rossiyans again attack Constantinople.

907 Hungarian horsemen, the Magyars, launch raids in Moravia, Germany and Italy.

910 The Byzantine emperor pays 'tribute' to the Magyars – creating one of the first international protection rackets.

913 Byzantines decline to pay tribute to Symeon of Bulgaria – he raids through Thrace and Macedonia, but is repulsed when he attempts to take Constantinople.

916 Bloody skirmishes around Anzio, another small town that, like Cambrai, will recur as an influential battlefield. The Saracen army is mauled by papal militia, and the Arabs expelled from central Italy.

917 Supported by some of the best heavy cavalry in the known world, Symeon I, of the Rhodopi Planina, assumes the title 'Czar of the Bulgarians and Greeks'. The Bulgarian Church separates from Rome and then from Constantinople. Symeon builds and trains his armies with serious intentions of world conquest.

924 Symeon devastates Greece and again threatens Constantinople. It is possible that Symeon's cavalrymen were the first to use spurs.

926
Guthfrith is driven out of York, then out of Northumbria, by Athelstan, who annexes his realm. The kings of Wales, Strathclyde and of the Picts and Scots submit and pay tribute to him.

929 Bloody *coup d'état* in Bohemia. 'The Good King', Wenceslas, is murdered by reactionary aristocrats, led by his brother, Boleslav.

934 Revolts, too, in Norway, against the cruel and violent King Eric Blodöye ('Bloodaxe', after the king's favourite weapon used to personally dispatch his opponents).

937 The Battle of Brunanburh. The Saxons defeat the Vikings and Celts.

938 Conflict in China. Khitans leave the old Ch'in capital on the Liaotung river, deserting the Wang Chien monarchy. They settle a fortress-site as a new capital at Yenching, later westernized as 'Peking' and latterly known as Beijing.

939 Arabs are ousted from Madrid by besieging forces from the Spanish kingdom of Léon.

940 Armed revolts against imperial rule in Japan start a period of violent turbulence, which grows into civil wars lasting two and a half centuries.

941 Russians yet again attack Constantinople, this time from the sea. Their fleet is bloodily repulsed.

950 Europe descends into 'the Dark Ages' of brutality and ignorance, fuelled by innumerable local wars in which there is no clear victor – or even a cause to fight for.

961 The Byzantine navy reconquers Crete from Arab occupation.

> *“ [The Byzantine] commanders had towers and siege weapons and flame-throwing tubes which could engulf 12 men at once, so fierce and adherent that none could withstand it ”*

Ibn al-Athir, Arab Muslim historian.

964 The fleet moves on to reclaim Cyprus.

970–971 The Russians are defeated at the battles of Presthlava and Dorystolum – and are driven out of the Balkans.

980 The renewal of Danish raids on England: they attack Chester, Thanet and Southampton.

982 Further violent Danish raids launched in Dorset, Portland and South Wales.

983
Erik the Red establishes Viking colonies in Greenland.

991 The Battle of Maldon. Byrhtnoth of Essex is crushed by the Danes on estuarine mud: more of his fighters are killed by drowning and suffocation than by blades.

994 Arabs destroy the monastery of Monte Cassino.

996 Quarrels among our friends in the north: Viking colonialists in Iceland move on and into the lands seized by Viking colonialists in Greenland. Armed skirmishes ensue as both parties assert their 'property rights'.

998 The Danes attack the Isle of Wight.

999 The Poles conquer Silesia.

1000

The end of the first millennium provokes, just as it would at the end of the second, widespread fear of the End of the World and the Last Judgement. The turning calendar for both millennia is marked with bangs and whimpers: in 1000, Chinese chemists perfect their invention of gunpowder, made up of charcoal, sulphur and potassium nitrate. In 2000, Australian fireworks operators will use this Chinese legacy to simulate a cascade of flowing fire from the Sydney Harbour Bridge.

1000 Saxons settle in Bristol.

1003 War between Germany and Poland. The Arabs sack Pisa.

1007 Ethelred II, son of Edgar the Peaceable, pays £30,000 to the Danes in return for a promise of two years' freedom from attacks.

1011 Ethelred invades South Wales. The Danes take advantage of his inattention to seize again the renewed riches of Canterbury.

1012 Ethelred pays another £48,000 to the Danish King Sweyn, with the understanding that he will remove his armed men from Kent.

1013 The Danes use their recent financial windfalls to re-equip many of their ships and to buy livestock, including most of the fast horses available. By autumn, Sweyn is master of all England: Ethelred flees to Normandy.

1014 Sweyn dies, and is succeeded by Knut (Canute). This marks the end of Norse rule in Ireland. The Celts are victorious at the Battle of Clontarf.

The Byzantine army wins an equally decisive campaign in western Bulgaria, taking tens of thousands of prisoners of war, all of whom are blinded on the orders of Emperor Basil II.

Heavy cavalry, including armoured knights, dominate the 11th century. Spurs are used. The knight's mail shirt (the byrnie) becomes longer and closer fitting; sleeves are extended from bicep area to wrist and the hem drops from just above the knee to just below the knee. Knights begin wearing the gambeson, a quilted leather or canvas shirt worn under the mail, to absorb blows. Surcoats, a light garment, are used over the knight's mail. Hauberks are also used, they are knee-length mail coats split at the sides to allow the knight to ride his horse, and also had a mail hood. With the hauberk, a knight wore a pointed iron helmet (having a vertical nasal bar) and used a large kite-shaped shield. Also, an infantry development of vast and future influence towards the end of the 11th century, the longbow appears for the first time at Manzikert.

1016 Norman knights are operating in southern Italy, their appearance is influential, as is their use of tanks at Cambrai. The Arabs largely withdraw to Sardinia.

1018 The end of war between Germany and Poland (since 1003). No clear decision is reached about boundaries, resources or any other issues between the warring states.

The start of religious wars in India: forces led by Mahmud of Ghazni pillage the sacred city of Muttra.

1024 Mahmud's well-trained army storms Somnath, in Gujarat, India.

1028 Canute, Danish king of the Britons, invades Norway with a small raiding force.

1030 The Battle of Stiklestad: Canute's expeditionary army, augmented by local support, defeats and kills former Norwegian King Olaf Haraldsson.

1035 Canute divides his realm for his three sons: Sweyn takes Norway, Hardicanute is given Denmark and England goes to Harold (the First).

1039 Prince Gruffydd of Gwynedd and Powys defeats a vastly stronger English army trespassing and bullying in the mountains of North Wales.

1041 The Battle of Montemaggiore. Norman knights aid Lombards to defeat the Greeks. William, duke of Normandy, aka 'the Conqueror', understands that he has the weaponry to win any given contemporary battle, if he can bend its manpower to his will.

1047 William crushes his rebellious nobles, most of them accoutred as armoured knights, at Val-des-Dunes. He is now sole commander of the most powerful heavy cavalry in Europe, and begins to develop a theoretical framework for their most effective use.

1050s William authorizes his fleet to probe and land raiding parties across the Channel. He also supports an expeditionary/combat-training force under Robert Guiscard, in southern Italy, where Norman hegemony is soon established.

1054 Alarmed by Norman military readiness and expansionism, Henry I of France launches a punitive strike into Norman history. William's knights destroy the French forces at Mortemer.

1056 Under torture, and solely to protect his people from further English predation, Gruffydd, prince of Cymru, does nominal homage to Harold of Wessex, heir to the English throne, and to Leofric of Mercia.

1057 Bitter civil wars in Scotland. King Macbeth, who had murdered his predecessor, Duncan, in 1040, is himself cut down by Duncan's son, Malcolm, who then loses the election for the throne to Macbeth's stepson, Lulach.

1058 Supported by a Northumbrian mercenary army, Malcolm seizes the throne against the will of Scotland's nobility, and has Lulach beheaded.

1061 Malcolm invades Northumbria at the head of an army largely trained by officers from both Siward and Tostig, generals and earls of Northumbria. The Scots army is, however, repulsed.

1062 The Normans complete the conquest of Messina, in Sicily, after a complex amphibious invasion using basal Roman designs of boat ramps, vastly increased in size and strength, to land heavy cavalry.

1063 In an uneasy alliance, Harold of Wessex pincer-moves forces with Tostig of Northumbria to subdue resistance movements in Wales.

1066 **January**: Harold II becomes king following the death of Edward the Confessor. His ally from the previous year's Welsh campaign, Tostig, now joins another coalition – with the Norwegian king, Harald Hardrade. Over 200 Viking ships, supported by Tostig's small fleet and battle-hardened army, make landings in the Tyne & Wear estuaries. **September**: At the battle known as Stamford Bridge, fought on 25 September, Harold's Saxon/English army defeats the Northmen's joint land forces and burns many of their ships; only 24 return to Norway. This effectively ended the Viking threat to English kingdoms forever. However, the clear and present danger lay elsewhere: William of Normandy had landed his disciplined troops at Pevensey, Sussex, on 28 September.

1066

October: After a desperate forced march from Yorkshire, Harold brings the invaders to battle at Hastings on 14 October, by which time the Norman knights were fully prepared. Harold is killed, according to some accounts, like the Bayeux tapestry, by an arrow, which penetrates his eye. The exhausted Saxon army is slaughtered, scattered, surrendered and the Norman knights ride unopposed to London.

December: William I, the Conqueror, is crowned 'King of All England' on Christmas Day.

1068 The Normans crush nationalist risings in the north and west of England. There is fighting near both Stamford Bridge and Edington, Wiltshire – both scenes of previous battles.

1070 Another rising, this time in the eastern flatlands, near the Isle of Ely, is led by Hereward the Wake: it is crushed by Norman soldiers wearing chain mail gauntlets – the original 'iron fist'.

1071 Normans conquer the final Byzantine holdings in Italy. Shortly thereafter, Robert Guiscard's Norman army in Sicily secures the port of Palermo, the last Byzantine presence on the island.

The Byzantine emperor is defeated and captured at Manzikert. The Turks invade Asia Minor.

In 1078, Emperor Michael VII Ducas collects the remaining soldiers from the former provinces of Asia Minor into a new body of cavalry – the so-called 'Immortals'. However, even though he supplements them with new recruits, they number only 10,000. They are the survivors of what had once been 21 themes, a force most likely well above 80,000 men.

1078
The building of the Tower of London begins (completed about 1298).

1087 William the Conqueror dies. He is succeeded by both his sons: Robert, who becomes ruler and duke of Normandy and Rufus, who will rule England as William II. The Norman war machine is unaffected, reaching out even as far as Rome to free Pope Gregory VII when he is imprisoned in the Castel Sant'Angelo by the Holy Roman Emperor, Henry IV. Robert Guiscard, who conducts the rescue mission, later dies a loyal Norman hero.

1091 By the Treaty of Caen, King William II and Duke Robert resolve upon returning the Holy Land to Christian rule, and so the Crusades are born.

1093 Malcolm of Scotland attempts another ill-advised invasion of England. He is killed as his undisciplined infantry are crushed at the Tyne, and succeeded by his brighter brother, Donald Bane.

El Cid

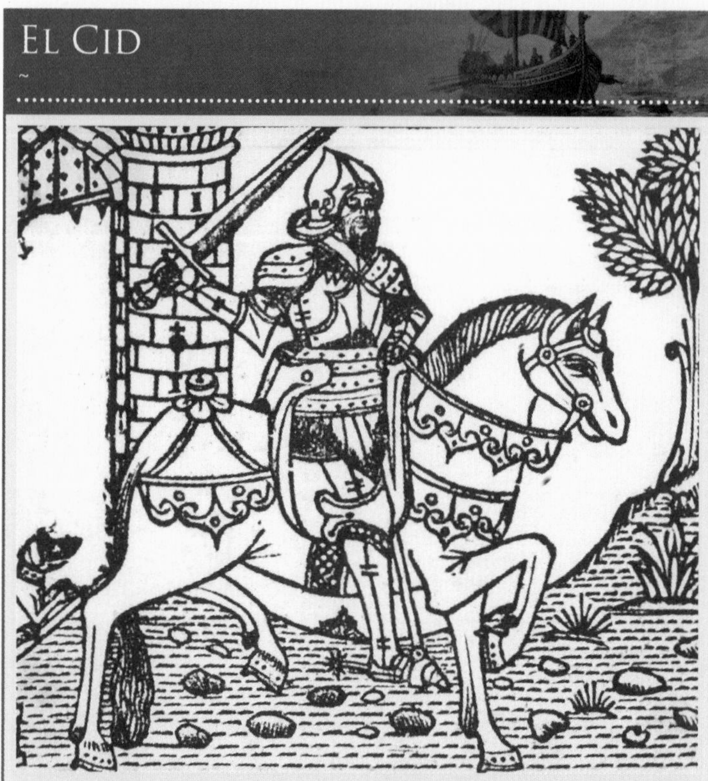

'El Cid', means 'chief', or 'lord', and was the Saracen's nickname for Rodrigo Dias de Bivar, in recognition of his skills on the battlefield. The Spanish called him Campeador, which means 'Champion', and this moniker all but sums up how they saw him. Dias was born in 1040, in Vivar, near Burgos, Spain, to a Spanish nobleman, Diago Lainez. He spent his youth in the service of Sancho, the eldest son of King Ferdinand. When Ferdinand died, his kingdom was divided between his three sons, but Sancho was not interested in sharing sovereignty and attacked his brothers and sisters. Dias was chosen to command his armies, and he did so with such success that Sancho was victorious. Sancho II died, childless, in 1072, and his brother, Alfonso VI, who had been exiled to Toledo, became king. Despite the fact that Dias had fought against him, Alfonso recognized a great warrior when he saw one, and made an effort to get him on side. He even married Dias to his sister, Jemina, in order to cement his loyalty.

Like many great warriors, Dias was a maverick. He fell out of favour with King Alfonso, and, seeking protection, offered his services to the Ruler of Sargossa in north eastern Spain, the Arabic leader al-Mu'tamin. He continued to work for Mu'tamin and his successor al- Msta'in for almost a decade. Dias eventually returned to work for Alfonso, but he didn't stick around for long. He was hoping to play Alfonso and the Moors off one another in order to weaken both armies. El Cid had his sights set on Valencia.

Gradually Dias tightened his grip on Valencia, and when its leader was killed by a protesting mob in 1092, Dias saw his chance and took it. He laid siege to the city, and two years later, entered Valencia as its conqueror.

Technically, El Cid ruled Valencia for Alfonso, but by this time he had become so powerful, and had such support from the Moors, that the King could barely intervene. El Cid began to behave like a king; he appointed his own bishops and married both of his daughters to royal princes. He lived out the rest of his life as the ruler of Valencia, and when he died, of natural causes, in 1099, his remains were interred in the monastery of San Pedro de Cardena near his hometown in Castille.

1094 'El Cid Campeador', aka Rodrigo Diaz de Vivar, captures Valencia from the Moors.

1095 Council of Clermont: Pope Urban II proclaims the first Crusade.

> ***" Let those who were brigands become soldiers of Christ; let those who have been fighting against their own brothers and relations now rightfully fight barbarians; let those who recently were hired for a few pieces of silver, win their eternal reward! Let those who have wearied themselves to the destruction of body and soul now work for the honour of both "***

Pope Urban II, at Clermont, 1095.

1096 Godfrey of Bouillon, duke of Lorraine, leads the first Crusader army, with Tancred, nephew of Robert Guiscard, as his second-in-command.

1097 Godfrey defeats the Turkish army at Dorylaeum and conquers Nicaea.

1098 The Crusaders again defeat the Turks at Antioch.

1099 The Crusaders take Jerusalem. Godfrey is appointed 'Defender of the Holy Sepulchre'. He moves to defeat an Egyptian army at Ascalon, where he dedicates the victory to El Cid, who has died, probably of a heart attack, in Valencia. Legend has it that El Cid's wife, Jimena, who would rule for two more years after his death, had his body strapped to his great warhorse, Babieca, and sent back into battle against an Almoravid force besieging Valencia. Legend says that Babieca (Spanish for 'stupid') trampled so many of the Almoravid Berber soldiers that the remainder took to their boats and sailed back to Mauritania. In the keening 'Song of the Cid' (*Cantar de mio Cid*), Babieca was never ridden again, lived to be forty years old and was buried with his master at Burgos Cathedral.

1100 William Rufus breaks his neck while hunting in the New Forest. Some say that his horse stumbled on a molehill, others that Sir Walter Tyrel shot at the king, or at his horse – some say accidentally, others that his arrow was deliberately aimed from a nearby grassy knoll. The most scurrilous suggest that Tyrel was in the pay of William II – Rufus's brother, Robert, duke of Normandy. Robert certainly seized the opportunity to invade England along much the

1101 The Treaty of Alton. Rufus's son, King Henry the First of England, buys off his uncle with most of his father's treasure – 'Bob's your Uncle' (the original usage for such a quick deal) – and Robert returned with his army to Caen.

1103 A vain attempt by Magnus III of Norway to reclaim an Irish kingdom. Celts kill him, take his boats and absorb many of his men into the Irish agricultural and fisheries workforce.

1104 Acre is taken by Crusaders – a secure port and fortified city in which Norman engineers immediately strengthen the defences.

1115 The state of Ch'in is formally established across the entire northern half of the current People's Republic of China.

Fortifications, especially of well-situated castles, become immensely strong during the 12th century. The trebuchet, a counterpoise siege engine, is used – able to throw a vastly heavier ball (rock, metal, pitch-fire) than the old siege-catapult. Cavalry equipment is also much refined during the 12th century. The war saddle, with high, wraparound cantle and pommel, secured to the horse with a double girth, is being used. Size and power of warhorses, and the quality of personal armour, have been steadily improved. Casque, or pot helm, is used. The casque had a flat top and nasal protection, which covered the entire face. It was extremely heavy, so sometimes a mail coif with padding, an iron cap and/or an iron visor was used instead. Towards the end of the century, a rigid back plate is added to knightly armour, to add protection during a head-on impact.

1135 Henry I dies. The English barons recognize his daughter, Matilda, as the natural successor. She asserts her right to become monarch after Stephen of Boulogne, a grandson of William the Conqueror, seizes the throne on the basis of his superior gender.

1138 David I of Scotland invades England in support of Matilda, and is defeated at the Battle of the Standards.

1139 Matilda lands at Arundel from Anjou with a Plantagenet army. Civil war begins in England.

1141 Matilda is proclaimed queen, at Winchester.

1145 Pope Eugene III proclaims the second Crusade.

"I open my mouth, I spoke; and at once the crusaders have multiplied to infinity. Villages and towns are now deserted. You will scarcely find one man to every seven women. Everywhere you see widows whose husbands are still alive"

St Bernard to Pope Eugene III

1147 Queen Matilda's support crumbles, and she leaves England. The Crusader army perishes in Asia Minor (Turkey). The Crusaders are victims of disease, thirst and continuous skirmishes with Muslim guerrillas. Only Frederick, duke of Swabia, emerges with any credit, rescuing the German king, Conrad III, in a fighting retreat and rearguard action.

1154 Stephen dies. He is succeeded by Matilda's son, Henry II, who institutes the Plantagenet dynasty, which will rule England until 1485.

1155
The birth of Genghis Khan, who will become the world's most successful cavalry commander.

1157 War in Scandinavia: the Christian King Eric of Sweden invades Finland and seizes control of 'pagan land'. Eric IX Jedvardsson is credited with the conversion of Finland to Christianity, albeit through the armed missionary zeal of Henry of Uppsala. Eric was less successful with the pagan Danes, whose troops rushed upon him at prayer in church on Ascension Day, 1160, and chopped him to pieces. The martyred Eric became as close to a 'patron saint' as is known in Swedish national life.

1162 Frederick I Barbarossa, king of Germany, the sole hero of the second Crusade, launches a massive attack on the republican stronghold of Milan. He burns most of the city and immediately marches on Venice, also known for its anti-imperial citizenry, who appeal, arbitrarily, for help from Byzantium.

1167 Frederick is crowned Holy Roman Emperor. He orders the rebuilding of Milan and enters into negotiations with fellow Swabian Welf VI to 'buy' Tuscany, Spoleto, Sardinia and Corsica. This vast purchase was disconcerting to both the Lombard League and the Grand Council of Venice, who both felt that they owned much of the land involved.

1176 The Battle of Legnano. Lombard League and allies defeat Barbarossa's army. Frederick negotiates the Peace of Venice and continues to expand his armed forces.

1183 Saladin takes Aleppo.

1187 Saladin defeats the Crusaders at Hittin, and takes control of Jerusalem.

1190 Frederick Barbarossa drowns in the river Saleph, in Cilicia, Anatolia. He leaves his son and successor, Henry VI, the most mobile and well-trained army in Europe.

> ***"Look at the state of the country, ruined and trampled under foot, at your subjects, beaten down and confused, at your armies, exhausted and sick, at your horses, neglected and ruined. There is little forage, food is short, supply bases are far away, the necessities of life are dear"***

Saladin, 1192

1193 Henry takes Richard I of England as a prisoner from the duke of Austria and releases him. Richard, known as 'The Lionheart' (though, as he spoke little or no English, more obviously as *Coeur de Lion*), reckoned that he could fight a Crusade with one hand behind his back. But he was really a man of straw. In the 10 years he 'ruled' England, he wore his tin armour to Cyprus, where he duped the local populace into allowing him to sell the entire island to the Knights Templar. He was captured twice, released twice and crowned twice.

1199 Richard *Coeur-d'étain*, Dick de Jaune-Paille, dies while conducting a siege in France, leaving his throne to his brother John, aka 'Lackland', and his realm to a most surprising group of erstwhile robber-barons.

1200 There are further developments in military technology during the 13th century: mail mesh is made fine enough to make chain mail gloves. Mail protection for horses becomes common. Torsion siege engines are used. Broad-beamed ships with rigging are developed. The fore and aft castles of ships become part of the main hull. For some sturdy infantrymen, thin plates begin to be worn with chain mail. Most horsemen wear the cuirass, a breastplate, followed by the use of a back-plate as well (perhaps to balance pectoral weight). By the 1290s, plate armour begins to be used on the extremities and joints. Shields become smaller, stronger and much lighter.

1202 Boniface of Montferrat leads the fourth Crusade. Venice provides ships for Frankish and Norman knights to attempt the recapture of Constantinople.

1203 The knights scatter the Byzantine mercenary army. Only the Varangians fight to protect the emperor, a defiance revered by Napoleon among many other military men.

THE VARANGIAN GUARD
1203

The Varangian Guard, also known as the Waring Guard or the Barbarian Guard, emerged in the 11th century, in Constantinople, as the bodyguard to the Byzantine emperor. The first mention of this guard appears in 1034, and Romanus IV reorganized them in the mid 11th century. Mostly, this bodyguard consisted of Danes and Englishmen. Many of the latter joined after the defeat at Hastings in 1066, preferring service to the emperor to life under Norman rule back home in England. The Varangians were ferocious fighters. They used the two-handed battleaxe as their preferred weapon (which is why they were also known as the 'axe-bearers' in Constantinople). They lived under their own laws, prayed at their own church and elected their own officers. Their leader was known as the 'Acolyte' (the follower), which was derived from the fact that he always followed immediately behind the emperor wherever he went. At banquets or audiences, the acolyte was found standing right behind the emperor's throne. Unlike bodies such as the Praetorian Guard, the Varangians became famed for their loyalty to the emperor, even their willingness to fight to the death to protect him. In 1203 they did just that.

1204 Crusaders complete the conquest of Constantinople and establish the Latin Empire.

1209 The beleaguered King John of England seeks to distract the private armies of his barons by invading Scotland. After a badly planned campaign he is excommunicated by Pope Innocent III.

1211 Genghis Khan, chief prince of the Mongols, invades China.

1213 King John submits to the pope, making England and Ireland into papal fiefdoms.

1214 Genghis Khan captures Peking.

> “ *I am the punishment of God, if you had not committed great sins, God would not have sent a punishment like me upon you* ”

Genghis Khan

1215
King John signs the Magna Carta, at Runnymede, limiting, among many other provisions, the King's right to wage unrestricted war.

1216 King John dies. A French force lands in England.

1217 The French are defeated at Lincoln and Sandwich. They retreat to their ships and leave.

1218 Genghis Khan captures Persia.

1223 Mongols invade Russian lands and win a huge battle in Ukraine.

1227 The death of Genghis Khan, first known as Temujin, and now more properly as Chinggis, meaning either 'Oceanic' or 'Resolute' ruler. He had been at war since 1207 in Tibet, and 1211 when he first took on the Chin dynasty. At his death, Mongol armies dominate from the Pacific Ocean to the Adriatic Sea. Tolui, his youngest son, inherit an army of 100,000 men, including most of the world's best cavalry.

1236 Arabs lose Cordoba to Castilian knights.

1237 Mongols secure Russia and occupy Moscow.

1240 The Crusade of Richard of Cornwall and Simon de Montfort: they retake the Saracen port of Jaffa.

Mongols, under the command of Batu Khan, whose father is Joshi, Genghis Khan's first son, take and sack Kiev.

1241 **March**: The battle of Chmielnick – Mongols defeat the feudal Polish army. **April**: The Battle of Liegnitz – the Mongols defeat the feudal Polish nobility and the Knights Templar; Battle of Mohi – Batu Khan and Subutai defeat Béla IV of Hungary; Battle of Sajo – the Mongols defeat Béla IV of Hungary.

1242 Batu Khan establishes his warriors – 'the Golden Horde' – at Sarai on the Lower Volga.

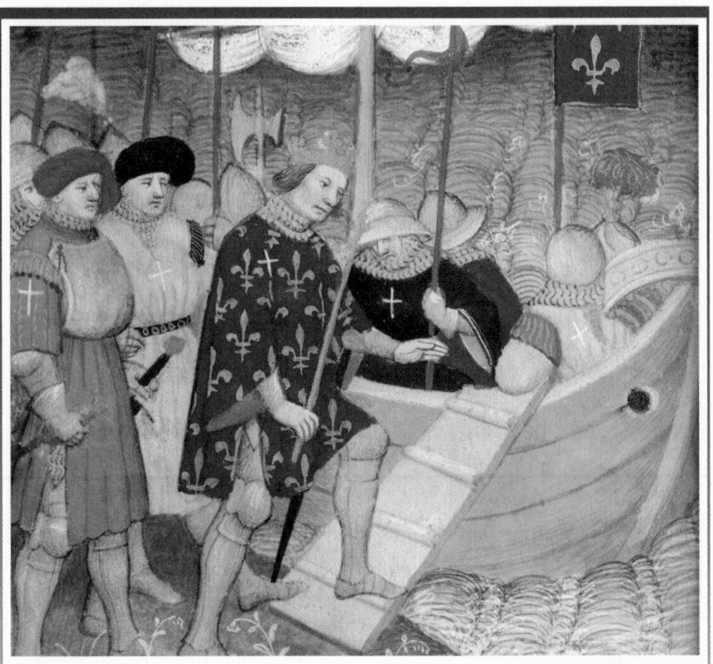

1249
Louis IX of France leads the seventh Crusade. He lands in Egypt, supported by some English-born Norman knights.

1250 The Saracens capture Louis IX and scatter his forces.

1251 Kublai Khan, grandson of Chinggis, secures his position as (Mongol) governor of China. He will head the barbarian Mongol Empire, with moderation and wisdom, from 1259 to 1294.

1254 The equally 'barbarian' Saracens of Palestine release the well-fed Louis IX into French custody.

1258 Mongols take Baghdad and overthrow the caliphate. The caliph is rolled up in a blanket, placed under a Persian rug, and then stamped to death.

1270 Louis IX, never a man to learn any lesson with celerity, sets off on the eighth Crusade.

1274 Kublai Khan sends a fleet to Japan; meeting concerted resistance, he withdraws.

1280 Kublai Khan founds the Yüan dynasty in China, which will outlive him, and last peacefully, until 1368.

1282 War of the Sicilian Vespers. Thousands of French citizens are massacred in Sicily and part of Naples. Taking advantage of the bloodshed and chaos, King Peter III of Aragon launches a successful invasion and annexes the island.

1287 Mongols invade Burma.

1291 The end of the Crusades. The last Crusader foothold in Palestine, at Acre, is lost.

1296 The coronation stone of Scotland is moved from Scone to Westminster after the good John Balliol resigns the Scottish crown to Edward I.

1297 Having lost their sacred coronation stone, the Scots form an army and smash the English at the Battle of Stirling Bridge. At much the same time, a sea battle is fought between the Genoese and the Venetians, off Curzola. The Genoese win.

1300 Edward I invades Scotland.

1306 Robert the Bruce, king of Scots, tries, and tries again, to defeat the English, but he is defeated at both Methuen and Dalry.

1314 The Battle of Bannockburn: Robert the Bruce's tartan army defeats the English under Edward II at Bannockburn.

> ***"Try, try and try again"***
>
> Robert Bruce

1315 The Swiss Battle of Morgarten demonstrates that an unarmoured man with a 2 m (7 ft) halberd can dispatch an armoured man-at-arms. Soon after, the Swiss begin using a 5.5 m (18 ft) pike and develop the pike square tactical formation, oddly reminiscent of the ancient Greek phalanx.

1326 Isabella, Edward II's wife, accompanied by her lover, Roger Mortimer, mounts an invasion of England and captures the king.

1327 Edward II is deposed by parliament and murdered at Berkeley Castle near Bristol. Edward III succeeds him. Walter de Millimete describes the earliest known gunpowder weapon. It was 1 m (3 ft) long with a 5 cm (2 in) bore diameter.

1337 Edward III decides he is also king of France. The French navy burns Portsmouth, so beginning the Hundred Years War.

1340 The English fleet defeats the French off Sluys; the French occupy Guienne and William Merlee of Oxford becomes the first weather forecaster to work with the military.

During the 107 years of the Hundred Years War, military equipment again pushes on. The empirical recipe for modern gunpowder is determined. A fixed rudder controlled by a tiller replaces the steering method of attaching an oar to the starboard side of a ship. Development of the compass and astrolabe allows for long-distance ocean voyages to be undertaken.

1357-1453

The English longbow achieves great victories in the Hundred Years War. Curved-keel ships, using one mast and sail, begin to be replaced by flatter ships with additional masts and sails. These new ships are faster and allow for greater use of artillery.

1346 The first recorded use of gunpowder in battle. The French are defeated at the Battle of Crécy by the more explosive 'English' longbow.

1356 Edward, 'the Black Prince', defeats the French at Poitiers, taking both King John II and his son, Philip, as prisoners.

1368 Local Ming insurgents overthrow the Mongol Yüan dynasty, established by Kublai Khan, after a brief and bloody civil war.

1370 The Black Prince sacks Limoges.

1371 The French army rallies, it cuts English supply lines, retakes Poitiers, then Angouleme and the vital port of La Rochelle.

1372 Owen-ap-Thomas, fighting with some noble, family and national entitlement as prince of Wales, aided by French ships, captures Guernsey from a surprised English garrison.

1381
English peasantry revolt against their rulers, led by Wat Tyler.

1385 The Portuguese use slings effectively against the Spanish. In the late 14th century, wrought-iron siege bombards, firing stone cannonballs of over 200 kg (450 lb), are being used.

1388 Scots peasants defeat an English army at Otterburn.

1394 King Richard II of England decides to invade Ireland.

1399 Richard II is deposed. Henry of Lancaster, aka Bolingbroke, succeeds to the throne of England as Henry IV. His son, also Henry of Monmouth, becomes the only Welsh-born 'Prince of Wales' since London monarchs stole the title.

1400 Honoré Bonet writes *Tree of Battles*, a chivalric attempt to define what may be permissible in war.

Bolingbroke's sons, Henry and John, respectively, gain victory at Shrewsbury against a wide coalition of British enemies – and then by deceit near York.

1410 Christine de Pisan, perhaps the first woman writer in history to support herself by her work, writes *The Art of Chivalry*.

1415 Henry of Monmouth, now Henry V, invades France. He takes Harfleur, Caen and Rouen; crushes the French aristocracy at Agincourt; then besieges and enters Paris.

"War without fire is like sausages without mustard"

Henry V, attrib.

1422 Henry V dies, succeeded by the 9-month-old Henry VI.
1428 Joan of Arc leads French armies against the occupying English.
1429 When Henry VI is crowned king of France at Westminster Abbey, London, Joan of Arc rescues her favourite Charles-Roi from a siege at Orléans and has him crowned, also as king of France, at Rheims Cathedral.
1431 Joan of Arc is burned at the stake in Rouen and Henry VI is again crowned king of France, this time in Paris. His hold on this title is about as secure as that of Louis IX, the later Bourbon.

JOAN OF ARC
1431

France was in a terrible state when Joan of Arc was born in January, 1412. At the time of her birth an unstable truce existed between France and England, but the fighting had ravaged France, and its people had not been allowed to recover from the Black Death of the previous century. The French population had been further damaged by the previous French king, Charles VI, whose frequent bouts of insanity meant he was often unable to rule.
Civil war erupted between two factions The Orleanist, or Armanac faction, led by Duke Charles D'Orleans, and their rivals, the Burgundians, who were led by Duke John of Burgundy. King Henry V of England soon stole the opportunity to reclaim the French throne for himself. His armies invaded in August of 1415.

Joan began to experience visions in 1424, when she was just 12 years old. At first they merely told her to be good and attend church regularly, but as Joan grew older the visions took on a new element. They began to instruct her in the ways of war, and persistently called for her to go to the local commander at Valonceurs, and obtain a guard to take her to the Royal Court. On 12 October 1428, the English besieged Orleans, the last major city in Charles's territory. The fate of the entire kingdom relied on that of Orleans. It looked, at this point, as if the Armanacs were finally beaten. Then along came Joan.

Once in the company of the dauphin, Joan asserted that she had been sent by God to defeat the English. She impressed Charles, and following rigorous testing of her abilities and her orthodoxy, she was given a suit of armour, and sent on a relief mission to the besieged city of Orleans. The extent of Joan's military skill and command is still a subject for debate between historians, but she was certainly able to inspire her army with a religious zeal, which spurred them on to victory in the battle for Orleans. After only nine days the siege was lifted. Several more victories led to Charles's coronation as the King of France, and a result of her military successes, 'the virgin of Orleans' has become a global icon.

1453 Finally, the Hundred Years War comes to an end. The English give up all French possessions, except Calais. The Byzantine (or eastern Roman) Empire also comes to an end. Ottoman Turks capture and kill the last emperor, Constantine XI, in his palace in Constantinople.

1455 Richard, duke of York, is named Lord Protector of England during the illness of Henry VI. He clashes with supporters of Edward, Henry's son, the prince of Wales. Richard, duke of York and his ally Richard Neville defeat Royalist forces at the Battle of St Albans. So begins the Wars of the Roses.

1456 The Turks, having ended Byzantine civilization, now set out to destroy Greece, home of democracy. They capture Athens and their army rolls on through Macedonia and Serbia, pausing only to tear down most of the Acropolis.

Prince Janõs Hunyady dies while using new 'armoured horses' and 'exploding shot' to drive the Turks back from Belgrade.

1471 Yorkists (represented by the white rose) gain ascendancy over Lancastrians (represented by the red rose) in the Wars of the Roses. Edward IV (a Yorkist) defeats and kills Richard, earl of Warwick (a Lancastrian) at the Battle of Barnet. Edward IV then proceeds directly to Gloucestershire where he defeats Queen Margaret's army (Lancastrians) and kills Prince Edward (Henry VI's son, Lancastrian). He then returns to London via Ealing in the west to the Tower, where he has Henry VI murdered.

1483 Edward IV dies. He is succeeded by his young son, Edward V. Duke Richard of Gloucester, is named as his Protector. Edward V (Yorkist) and his little brother (also duke of York) then disappear, probably murdered by their uncle Richard (soon to be Richard III) in the Tower of London. This enrages the Lancastrians, who call on Henry Tudor, earl of Richmond for help.

1485 Henry Tudor lands at Milford Haven in south-west Wales. He recruits enough Welsh archers on his march to the English midlands to defeat Richard III at the Battle of Bosworth Field, with the help of turncoat cavalry under Lord Stanley of Derby, who came to Leicestershire to support the king, but changed his mind when the Cwmraeg arrows started flying.

1492 Completion of 'Reconquista': Spanish armies, consolidated under the monarchy of Ferdinand of Aragon and Isabella of Castile, drive the Arabs from Granada and so extinguish the Moorish kingdom. Christopher Columbus begins his journey to America.

Henry Tudor, now Henry VII, invades France.

EARLY MODERN WARFARE

1494–1648

1494 By the treaty of Tordesillas, Spain and Portugal divide the entire New World between them, as Vasco da Gama reaches India by sea.

Meanwhile, 'the imposter' Perkin Warbeck, still pretending to be the younger of the 'Little Princes in the Tower' and calling himself 'Richard IV', attracts support in Italy, Scotland, Kent, Ireland and Cornwall.

1495 Sir William Stanley, Lord Chamberlain to Henry VII, decides to support Warbeck. He is executed under a new English statute of treason.

1497 Warbeck lands in Cork from Scotland, then lands in Cornwall, tries to take Exeter, then Taunton, where he is captured by Tudor militia and imprisoned in the Tower of London.

1499 Warbeck is hanged at Tyburn.

Much bigger wars between Swiss cantons and the Swabian League and Ottomans versus Venice. The Peace of Basel secures Helvetian independence and perpetual prosperity. The Venetian fleet is defeated at Sapienza: Lepanto surrenders to the sultanate.

1500 Pope Alexander VI proclaims a year of Christian Jubilee: an extra tithe (one-tenth of all income) is imposed on Christendom to fund a crusade against the Turks.

1501 Henry VII of England makes two decisions in favour of peace rather than war: he declines the pope's request to lead the putative Crusaders, and his older son, Arthur, marries Catherine of Aragon, to cement an Anglo-Spanish alliance.

1502 Prince Arthur dies, aged 16.

1503 Henry, now prince of Wales, later Henry VIII, becomes engaged to marry Catherine of Aragon – the first step towards the most fundamental split in European history, between Catholicism and what will become Protestant reform. Most of the wars of empire, religion, colonialism and rage seem to stem from this betrothal and the failure of the subsequent marriage. Henry renounced the marriage contract in 1505, and became engaged to Margaret of Austria in 1506; yet, at the age of 18, in 1509, after his father's death, he married Catherine as originally planned.

1511 Pope Julius II forms the Holy League with Venice and Aragon to drive the French out of Italy. Henry VIII joins England to the League and begins to reform the Royal Navy.

1512 The French defeat the Spanish and papal forces at Ravenna, with Pierre du Terrail, as hero of the battle.

1513 James IV of Scotland is killed at the Battle of Flodden Field. His infant son, as James V, succeeds him for whom his mother, Queen Margaret (Tudor) acts as regent. It is through this line that James VI and I will unite Scotland with the English throne.

The Royal Navy builds the first double-deck ships of 1,000 tons, carrying 70 guns.

1515 France has the first nationalized armaments industry. King Francis I is victorious at the Battle of Marignano, and conquers Milan.

1517 The Turks take Cairo and rule both Upper and Lower Egypt. Salim I extends his suzerainty over all of Arabia, after Mecca surrenders to him.

1520 Niccolo Machiavelli writes *The Art of War*, including the 'Italian system' of fortification. The sunken profile of fortresses has become well established as a military engineering technique. Armour has become merely ceremonial. The high level of masonic skill needed to carve properly shaped stone cannonballs makes the stone-throwing cannon obsolete.

Christian II, king of Denmark and Norway, learns Machiavellianism very quickly. After he defeats a Swedish army at Lake Asunden, he is crowned king of Sweden in Stockholm and grants full amnesty to all Swedish bishops and nobles, including Eric Vasa. Then he massacres all of them.

1521 Sultan Suleiman I ('the Magnificent') conquers Belgrade and orders his army on to Hungary. The Battle of Tenochtitlan: Spanish brigands seize the Halls of Moctezuma in pursuit of gold.

1522 Suleiman ejects the knights of St John from Rhodes.

War in the New World: Hernando Cortes assumes control of Mexico after destroying the Aztec state with gunpowder, terror and disease. His forces then 'conquer' Guatemala, achieving swift military superiority over native resistance armed only with fists, slings and miniature blowpipes.

THE SPANISH CONQUISTADORS
1522

The Spanish conquistadors saw their mission to explore and conquer new lands as a natural continuation of the Holy Crusades, fought by Roman Catholic soldiers under the guidance of the Vatican. Roman Catholic priests and friars accompanied the Spanish armies on all their missions to the New World, in order to help introduce the South American 'savages' to the Christian faith. The presence of these important religious figures must have lent precious validity to the young Spanish conquistadors and their captains, but their wealthy patrons had other things on their minds besides promoting the word of God. They were also motivated by wealth, power, prestige, improved trade opportunities and the building of a Spanish empire in a land that was hugely rich in resources such as gold, silver and spices. The Spanish wanted to introduce a feudal system known as encomienda to the people of the New World; this meant that they expected the native peoples to pay tribute to the Spanish in return for protection and religious instruction. The system of encomienda was utterly abused, and far from offering protection – the conquistadors brought slavery, oppression, pestilence and disease to the people of South America.

1525 The Spanish infantry become first to use muskets.

1526 Babar founds a Mogul dynasty in Delhi. It will last until 1761, bringing to India both cavalry and distance-communications to military effect for the first time.

1527 Chaos in Rome as imperial troops pillage the city, killing over 4,000 inhabitants, looting art treasures and inflicting widespread arson and rape. Pope Clement VII is imprisoned in Castel Sant'Angelo. Sometimes deemed 'the end of the Renaissance', and largely considered the nadir of the papacy as a military power.

1531 Religious civil war in Switzerland between Catholic cantons and Protestant Zurich. Forest cantons are defeated at the Battle of Kappel, where Protestant leader Huldrych Zwingli is killed. Hostilities are suspended soon afterwards because both sides were over budget.

1532
Francisco Pizarro leads Spanish gunmen on an expedition from Panama to Peru in search of further loot. Inca resistance improves. Aztecs use long-distance slingshots against the invaders. Pizarro will respond by executing thousands of Incas.

1539 Spain annexes Cuba, again with maximized bloodshed.

1541 Suleiman I takes the Danube city of Buda and annexes most of (modern) Hungary. (Turkish hegemony there until 1686.)

By the mid 16th century, English smiths develop a compact four-wheeled carriage for trunnion-equipped shipboard cannons. In 1543, the English develop reliable iron cannons; despite being heavier and bulkier than a bronze cannon, susceptible to internal corrosion and bursting like a bomb at failure, they were one-third as expensive to build as bronze cannons. Hand-held explosive weapons are also prone to bursting. Widespread military admiration for Aztecs and Incas effectively using slings against the Spanish conquistadors, sometimes out-ranging the muskets. Through to the 1580s, military planners argue over the relative use of longbows versus gunpowder weapons.

"At this time new Spain was extremely full of people, and when the smallpox began to attack the Indians it became so great a pestilence among them throughout the land that in most provinces more than half the population died... They died in heaps, like bedbugs. Many others died of starvation"

Fray Toribio Motolinia, c.1541, *History of the Indians of New Spain.*

1548 Gonzalo Pizarro, Francisco's bloodthirsty son, is defeated at the Battle of Xaquixaguane, in Peru, by Don Pedro de la Gasca.

1560 Turkish galleys defeat the Spanish fleet off Tripoli. The Spanish commander, duke of Medina, drowns when his ship is sunk.

1566 The Dutch revolt against the Spanish occupation of the Netherlands begins. Calvinists force abolition of the inquisition.

1567 The duke of Alba arrives as military governor and begins a reign of terror. Conquistador tactics of fear and brutality, developed in South America, are seen for the first time in Europe. Calvinist Counts Egmont and Hoorn are beheaded in Brussels. Dutch resistance hardens.

1571 Turks sack and burn Nicosia, Cyprus; declare war on the Venetian republic; then take Famagusta and massacre its inhabitants. It is possible that their urban warfare tactics are 'inspired' by the duke of Alba. A Venetian fleet under the command of Don Juan of Austria meets the Turks off Lepanto. In one of the most devastatingly decisive naval battles in history, the Turkish fleet is entirely destroyed: Ottoman naval power is broken.

1573
Dutch resistance for seven months in siege of Haarlem. When Alba's forces break through, Haarlem is a burned-out city of the dead.

1575 Mogul emperor Akbar conquers Bengal. His infantry may be the first fully amphibious land army.

1576 Spanish conquistadors sack Antwerp.

1577 Don Juan of Austria, new governor of the Netherlands, issues a 'Perpetual Edict' to settle 'this civil war'. It is flatly rejected by William of Orange, who marches with an army of Hollanders and Zeelanders on Brussels.

1578 Death of Don Juan: Elizabeth of England offers to mediate between Spain and the Dutch.

1579 The Treaty of Utrecht marks the foundation of the Dutch republic; Elizabeth signs a military alliance with William of Orange.

1580 In Russia, Czar Ivan 'the Terrible' strangles his rebellious son and heir with his own hands.

In Portugal, the duke of Alba, also the terrible, leads an annexing Spanish army.

1583 The Spanish burn Antwerp again. William of Orange accepts sovereignty over the northern Netherlands.

1584
Spanish hit man Balthazar Gérard assassinates William of Orange.
Ivan the Terrible (pictured) dies, probably assassinated by his younger son, Fyodor, who becomes czar, but immediately relinquishes most of his powers to his brother-in-law, Boris Godunov.
Maurice of Nassau assumes command of the Dutch army and vows to continue the struggle against the brutal Spanish occupation.

1585 Elizabeth Tudor is offered sovereignty over the Netherlands: she declines, but agrees to take the country under English protection, immediately ordering Francis Drake to attack Vigo and Santo Domingo from the sea.

1586 Pope Sixtus V promises financial support to send a Spanish invasion fleet against England and proclaims the deposition of the heretic Elizabeth as a Crusade.

THE SPANISH ARMADA
1588

The Spanish threat loomed large over England throughout the reign of Elizabeth I, finally culminating in the launch of the Spanish Armada in 1588. The reasons for the dispute centred on the fact that Elizabeth I was a Protestant monarch and Philip II a devout Catholic, who believed it was his religious duty to spread the faith wherever possible. At this time Spain had control of the Spanish Netherlands (modern day Holland and Belgium). Holland wanted independence from Spain, because Protestantism had secretly taken root in the country. The Spanish inquisition was active in all countries under Spanish rule, and this meant that Protestantism (not to mention any other religion apart from Catholicism) was a crime punishable by death. Under Elizabeth's reign, the English had been helping Protestants in Holland, and this infuriated Philip. He grew more determined to bring England under his control in order to secure the Spanish Netherlands and put a halt to the damage Francis Drake was doing to the Spanish silver trade in sinking their ships and capturing their cargo. The execution of Mary Queen of Scots in 1587 further exacerbated the hostilities between the two nations. Mary was also a Catholic, and had named Philip of Spain as her successor. By this time though, the preparation for an invasion was already well underway. When it finally set sail, the Spanish armada numbered 130 ships, making it easily the biggest naval fleet of its age. According to Spanish records over 30,493 men sailed in them – the majority of whom were soldiers. Many of the naval vessels had been converted from merchant ships, so they were not as splendid, or as well equipped as they appeared. These ships were large and extremely heavy, which made them difficult to manoeuvre – especially at speed. This did not strike the Spanish commanders as an immediate problem because they did not intend to engage in battle at sea. The ships in the armada were primarily designed to transport troops to England, where they would alight and fight. The English were better trained than their Spanish counterparts in combat at sea, and they had been busy while the Spanish prepared their ships. The English had set up a number of signal beacons on high ground around the English and Welsh coasts, so when the Spanish ships were finally sighted off the Lizard on 19 July 1588, the news immediately spread throughout the kingdom. The English ships slipped out of Plymouth harbour under cover of darkness, in order to meet the Spanish fleet at the battle of Gravelines.

> *"In our last fight with the enemy [The Spanish Armada]... we sunk three of their ships and made some...so leaky that they were not able to live at sea. After that fight, notwithstanding that our powder and shot was well near all spent, we set on a brag [bold] countenance and gave them chase as though we wanted [lacked] nothing, until we had cleared our own coast and some part of Scotland of them"*

Lord Howard of Effingham, commander of the English fleet, to Henry Walsingham, 7 August 1588.

1592 Hideyoshi of Japan attacks Korea, but is defeated at sea. The Korean victory heralds a new age of warfare, when the use of ironclad naval vessels gives the Korean fleet a vast advantage over the wooden Japanese ships.

1595 Spanish reprisals for the loss of their armada. They raid the Cornish ports of Penzance and Mousehole, burning several cottages and stealing several sheep.

1596 Drake sacks and burns the harbour of Cadiz. The Spanish take Calais.

1597 A second Spanish Armada sails for British invasion beaches: it is scattered by storms in the Bay of Biscay before Royal Naval ships can engage.

1600 Maurice of Nassau breaks the deadlock in the Spanish Netherlands. In a major battle at Nieuport, his Dutch army scatters a larger Spanish force under Archduke Albert.

In Japan, too, there is a major military resolution. Ieyasu Tokugawa, successor to the failed Hideyoshi, establishes himself as unquestioned ruler of the restored shogunate by crushing his rivals at Sekigahara. He moves his capital from Kyoto to Yedo (now Tokyo), and welcomes technical advice from the first English navigator to reach the Home Islands – his name is William Adams: he is a shipbuilder, and he has seen iron cladding techniques in Korea.

1602 The Spanish land soldiers and priests in Ireland, hoping to raise a Catholic revolt against Elizabeth and her Protestant successors, but are duped, then shepherded to surrender at Kinsala.

1603
Death of Elizabeth I, at the age of 70. Her very existence enraged Catholic Europe, but her death brought a United Kingdom very close. She left a navy, a nation and a developing empire that was in control of its own destiny.

1609 Finally, a truce is agreed between Spain and Holland, after 43 years of colonial struggle.

1611 The war of Calmar is declared, by Denmark, on Sweden. Gustavus II (Gustavus Adolphus) is elected king and immediately creates a professional army – in three years, Sweden has an advanced army based on its use of lighter muskets and cartridges, plus mobile artillery pieces that had been recently developed. The Swedes also use later innovations during the 17th century: the ring and socket bayonet is invented, bayonet use replaces the pike and the flintlock musket replaces the matchlock harquebus. Swedish officers are among the first to use telescopes, too.

1614 Gustavus Adolphus deploys his new army: he captures Novgorod from Russia.

1617 The 'Peace of Stolbov' ends war between Sweden and Russia. Gustavus recognizes Czar Michael; returns Novgorod, and obtains Karelia in exchange. The whole process stands as a model for adversarial settlements of military matters.

1618 The rumbling conflict between Catholic and Protestant, which led to the Dutch Revolt, the Spanish Armada and the Helvetian civil wars, flares in Prague and will ignite the Thirty Years War. Two holy Roman regents, Slawata and von Martinitz, are thrown from the town hall's windows by anti-imperial Hussites led by Matthias von Thurn. Both Catholics survive the defenestration and the 17 m (55 ft) fall. The pope will claim that angels brought them safely to ground. The Hussites point out they landed in a huge pile of pig manure. Because of such puerilities, an imperial army, under Count Karl Bucquoi, enters Bohemia to suppress von Thurn's rebels.

1619 Von Thurn marches on Vienna with an army of Bohemian patriots, receiving support from Bethlen Gabor of Transylvania who invades imperial territory in Hungary, captures Pressburg, crosses the Danube and also heads for Vienna.

1620 The Catholic League army under Count Tilly defeats Frederick's coalition at the Battle of the White Mountain near Prague. Bohemian revolt against Ferdinand is savagely suppressed with many executions and mass expulsions of all the leading rebels and Protestant clergy.

1621 This merely shifts the war from Bohemia to the Palatinate. Frederick is placed under ban-edict of the Holy Roman Empire – his defiance stirs further Protestant militancy elsewhere: French Huguenots rebel against the autocratic Louis XIII; the 12-year truce between Holland and Spain runs out – the war in the Netherlands resumes and German Protestant defiance of Count Tilly causes him to order the destruction of the library of Heidelberg University and the burning of all of its books.

Raimondo Montecuccoli
1621

Raimondo, Count of Montecuccoli, was born to Burgundian parents on 21 February 1609, at the castle of Montecuccoli in Modena, in northern Italy. Raimondo's uncle, Count Earnest Montecuccoli, was a distinguished Austrian general, and, at the age of 16, Raimondo joined his regiment. In the years that followed, Raimondo saw a great deal of active service in the Low Countries and Germany. He rose quickly through the ranks to become a captain of the infantry before going on to fight in the storming of New Brandenburg, the first battle of Breitenfeld and at Lützen. As a lieutenant-colonel of the cavalry he fought in the battle of Nordlingen, and at the storming of Kaiserslauten – where he showed unusual brilliance and found himself promoted again – this time to the rank of colonel. As a colonel he fought in Pomerania, Bohemia and in Saxony, at the surprise of Wolmirstadt, as well as the battles of Wittstock and Chemnitz. In 1639 he was taken prisoner at Melnik and detained in Stettin and Wiemar. Whilst a prisoner of war, Montecuccoli studied extensively – his chosen subjects included military strategy, but also geometry, history and architecture. It was here that he planned his great project; an attempt to formulate a general theory of war. His endeavours culminated in the publication of three major works: *Treatise on War (Trattato della Guerra)*, *On the Art of War (Del Arte Militare)* and the celebrated *On War against the Turks in Hungary (Della Guerra col Turco in Ungheria)* or *Aphorisms*. Montecuccoli has become famous for pointing out one major pitfall of modern warfare, he noted 'For war, you need three things. 1. Money, 2. Money, 3. Money'.

1622 Tilly is defeated at Wiesloch, but wins twice, with much gratuitous bloodshed, when he splits the forces of Georg-Frederic of Baden (crushed at Wimpfen) from the larger army of Christian of Brunswick, which is ground down at the Battle of Höchst.

1623 Tilly's Spanish army defeats another German force under Christian of Brunswick at Stadtlohn, and advances deep into Westphalia.

1624 England declares war on Spain.

1625
Tilly (pictured) invades Lower Saxony; Spanish General Ambrogio Spinola breaks an 11-month siege and takes Breda from the Dutch; Emperor Ferdinand II appoints Albrecht von Wallenstein, duke of Friedland.

1626 Wallenstein defeats Mansfield of Halle at Dessau and begins a long pursuit of Mansfield's disintegrating army into Silesia and as far as Hungary.

1627 The English Navy fails to relieve Huguenots at La Rochelle. Wallenstein conquers Silesia, while Tilly seizes Brunswick. Imperial forces occupy Mecklenburg and Jutland.

1628 Wallenstein is created duke of Mecklenburg and lord high admiral of the Baltic. King Christian IV of Denmark appeals to Sweden for help. Gustavus Adolphus enters the war by raising Wallenstein's siege of Stalsund.

1630 Gustavus Adolphus marches into Germany. Wallenstein declines battle against the superior Swedish forces and is dismissed by the emperor. Tilly is handed imperial high command.

1631 German Protestant princes ally themselves with Sweden. Tilly moves swiftly to wipeout the small Swedish garrison at Neu Brandenburg, then moves on to burn Magdeburg and Halle before invading Saxony. John Georg, elector of Saxony, asks the Swedes for help. Gustavus Adolphus amputates Tilly's over-extended forces at Breitenfeld.

1632 Wallenstein is reinstated as imperial commander. Tilly is mortally wounded and his army is scattered by the Swedes at the Battle of the Lech. Gustavus Adolphus outmanoeuvres Wallenstein at Nuremberg and Munich, and then decisively defeats him at Lützen. Gustavus is wounded in action with his lancers, allowing Wallenstein to withdraw. When Gustavus dies, the Swedish army is unable to rally.

1634 Wallenstein is assassinated. Matthias Gallas leads the imperial forces to victory at Nördlingen.

1635 John Georg of Saxony deserts his Swedish alliance.

1636 Swedish troops rally to defeat the Saxons (their former allies) at Wittstock.

1637 Another small Calvinist rally: the Dutch, under Frederick Henry of Orange, recapture Breda.

1639 'Bishops War' in Scotland. Charles I leads his army to York, but does not attack. Following the pacification of Berwick, Scottish episcopacy is abolished.

1640 Second Bishops War. The Scottish army crosses the Tweed and reaches the Tyne, defeating the king's army at Newburn. Treaty of Rippon: Charles agrees to pay the Scots £860 per diem, on the condition that they retreat.

1641 Thomas Wentworth, earl of Strafford, the king's chief adviser is beheaded to appease Parliamentary demands.

1642

Charles marches his guards to Westminster, intending to arrest six members of the House of Commons (pictured), and is repulsed. He retreats to Hampton Court and then to the Midlands. His Puritan opponents are encouraged by Protestant victories in Europe: four imperial armies are broken at battles of Wolfenbüttel, Kempten, Schweidnitz and Breitenfeld.

English Civil War becomes inevitable. The king's battle standard is raised at Nottingham. The Battle of Edgehill takes place.

THE ENGLISH CIVIL WAR
1642

Civil War in England began with the Bishop Wars, when King Charles I of England led his forces against the Scots, with the aim of forcing them to accept Anglican reforms to the church. His attempts failed, mainly because of lack of faith and funds, and he was forced to leave Scotland before he had even fought a battle. Unrest continued north of the border, and when Charles discovered that the Scots had been plotting with the French, he went to parliament to negotiate the funding for a full-scale invasion. Parliament would not give Charles the money he needed, so Charles dismissed them and went ahead with this military operation without their backing. The results were disastrous. The Scots defeated the English and stole the opportunity to take Northumberland and Durham in the process. In November 1640, Charles was humiliated into recalling parliament.

The general hostility between Parliament and the monarch continued until 4 January 1642, when Charles attempted to have five members of parliament arrested. Following this incident Charles left London, and both factions began stockpiling weapons and recruiting troops ready for battle. In August 1642, Charles began the war by raising his standard in Nottingham. At this stage, Parliament had no intention of killing the king, they simply wanted to rehabilitate Charles, and then reinstate him on the throne with a new pro-parliament attitude. The majority of English citizens were neutral in the wars – there were between 13,000 and 14,500 men actually fighting on each side. The royalists tended to be based in the North and West of England and in Wales, while Parliamentarians had more support in the richer South, including the capital – London. The parliamentarians were in a much better position than their Royalist rivals, they controlled most of the ports, since the merchants who owned them saw more opportunity to profit from a parliament-run government. In addition, parliament had access to more funds. They also had the power to collect taxes, while the King had to rely on the contributions of wealthy Royalists.

When fighting finally broke out, at the Battle of Edgehill on 23 October, 1642, both armies found they were fairly equally matched, and the result was bloody but inconclusive. Edgehill put an end to either side's hope for a quick victory, and triggered a full blown civil war which continued for a further four years, culminating with the execution of King Charles I and the abolition of the monarchy on 6 February 1649.

1643 At Bradford, the Royalists scatter Parliament's infantry and ride on to take Bristol. Oliver Cromwell resists at Grantham, his Roundhead cavalry score a victory against the king's superior army at Newbury. The Roundheads succeed at Leeds, Reading, Wakefield, Gainsborough and Gloucester.

> ***" I would rather have a plain russet-coated captain who knows what he fights for, and loves what he knows, than that which you call a 'gentleman' and is nothing else "***

Oliver Cromwell to Sir William Spring and Maurice Barrow, September 1643.

1644 The Siege of Lyme: a Parliamentary outpost in a mostly Royalist West Country. The Parliamentarians are able to retain access to the sea, and so are able to receive reinforcements and supplies from the Earl of Wessex' fleet. After two months the Royalists finally give up move on.

1645 **January**: Thomas Fairfax is appointed commander in chief; armistice talks open in Uxbridge. **February**: Battle of Inverlochy – the Covenanters are defeated by Montrose; the New Model Army is officially founded; Uxbridge armistice talks fail. **March**: Prince Rupert leaves Oxford for Bristol. **April**: A total of 150 Irish soldiers, who are on their way to serve for the Royalists under Charles, are captured at sea by Parliamentarians and slaughtered. **May**: The Battle of Auldearn – the Covenanters are defeated by Montrose. **June**: Prince Rupert's army sacks Leicester; Oliver Cromwell is officially named as the lieutenant-general of the cavalry; Battle of Naseby – Parliamentarian victory; Royalists lose Carlisle. **July**: Battle of Langport: Parliamentarian victory. **September**: Prince Rupert surrenders Bristol; Battle of Philliphaugh – Covenanters defeat Montrose at Selkirk; Battle of Rowton Heath – Parliamentarian victory. **October**: The crushing of Basing House.

1646 **February**: Battle of Great Storrington. **April**: Charles I flees Oxford. **May**: Charles I surrenders his forces at Scotland. **June**: Thomas Fairfax's New Model Army occupies Oxford. **July**: The English parliament sets the Newcastle Propositions for Charles I. **August:** Raglan Castle surrenders to General Thomas Fairfax after a three-month siege. The castle is destroyed.

1647 **March**: Bavaria, Cologne, France and Sweden sign the truce of Ulm. **August**: The New Model Army marches to London following a pay dispute; at the Battle of Dugan's Hill, Irish forces are defeated by English Parliamentarians. **November**: The Battle of Knocknanuss – the Irish forces are again defeated by Parliamentarians.

1648 **January**: The English parliament breaks off negotiations with Charles I, thereby beginning the second phase of the English civil war; The Dutch and the Spanish sign the treaty of Munster, ending the Eighty Years War. The Spanish Empire agrees to acknowledge the existence of the Dutch republic of the United Netherlands, which was once a province of Spain; The Khmelnytsky uprising takes place in present-day Ukraine. **April**: The Portuguese defeat the Dutch army in the north of Brazil**. October**: The Battle of Tippycart is fought in the New World; the treaty of Westphalia brings the Thirty Years War to an end. **November:** Pride's purge occurs in England, when colonel Thomas Pride launches a *coup d'état* (the only one of its kind ever to take place on English soil), leading to the creation of the Rump Parliament.

ENLIGHTENMENT

1649–1851

1649 **January**: King Charles I, of England, Scotland and Ireland, is beheaded; Prince Charles Stuart declares himself king of England, Scotland and Ireland, but none of the countries recognizes him as such. **February**: Scotland is the first of the three countries to recognize Charles II as king, and crowns him in his absence. **March**: In France, the Frondeurs and the French government sign the Peace of Rueil; in England, the House of Commons dismiss the House of Lords. **May**: The Rump Parliament declares England to be a commonwealth; Robert Blake becomes an admiral of the English fleet.

1649
August: Oliver Cromwell (pictured) invades Ireland, expels the papal nuncio and sacks Drogheda and Wexford.

1650 Charles II lands in Scotland.

1651 Charles II, king of Scotland, leads a Scottish army to Worcester, where Cromwell's cavalry annihilates it. Charles runs away before the battle is won or lost, and flees to France while the remainder of his family are sold into slavery.

1652 English and Dutch warships clash at the Battle of the Downs, off Folkestone, over trade monopolies. The English ships are heavier, faster and better armed. The Dutch fleet is scattered.

1653 Dutch ships are mauled in three successive battles, off Portland, North Foreland and Texel.

> **“*The English are about to attack a mountain of gold; we are about to attack a mountain of iron*”**

Adrian Pauw, grand pensionary of Holland, 1653

1654 The Dutch finally accept English merchant navy monopolies. War between Russia and Poland: Czar Alexis seizes Smolensk.

1656 'Northern War' spreads. Charles X of Sweden invades Poland, takes Warsaw and Krakow.

1657 Denmark attacks Sweden, taking advantage of the Polish War. Swedes also confronted by Russia, Prussia, Austria and Brandenburg.

1658 Oliver Cromwell dies. His son Richard succeeds him as Lord Protector. The Swedes make and break a peace treaty with the Danes: Copenhagen is besieged.

1660 Treaties of Oliva and Copenhagen resolve most Northern War disputes. The Swedes and the Russians fight on. Southern War in Transylvania. Prince Géorg Rákoczy is killed in battle against the invading Turks. Emperor Leopold I commits the Habsburg army to check the Turkish advance. Charles II returns to London.

1661 Peace of Kardis: Russia and Sweden end the 'Ice War'.

King John of Portugal gives Bombay to Charles I, as part of the dowry of his daughter, Catherine of Braganza. His negotiators fail to mention that drought has made most of India a vast famine zone.

1663 The Turks declare war on the Holy Roman Empire. They occupy Transylvania, invade Hungary and overrun the impregnable fortress of Nové Zamky in Slovakia.

1664 The Austrian army pinions the Turks against cliffs and bankside at St Gotthard. Thousands drown in the Raab river. The Turks sue for truce at Vasvar.

British troops invade the 'New Netherlands' and annex an area from Connecticut to Delaware. 'New Amsterdam' is renamed 'New York'.

1665 Combined British and Portuguese armies twice repel Spanish invaders at Montes Claros and Villa Viciosa, securing Portuguese independence and frontiers.

1666

June: Four Days Battle: the Dutch fleet defeats the English. **August**: St James's Day Battle: the English fleet defeats the Dutch; Rear Admiral Robert Holmes leads a raid on the Dutch island of Terschelling, destroying 150 merchant ships in the Vlie estuary, and pillaging the town known as West Terschelling.

1667 The Truce of Andrusovo ends the 13-year war between Russia and Poland: Kiev is ceded to Russia. 'War of Devotion' the French quarrel with Spain. French troops invade the Netherlands. With the Peace of Breda agreement, the French, Dutch and English end mutual hostilities.

1668 The Treaty of Lisbon: Spain recognizes Portuguese independence. Peace of Aix-la-Chapelle: Spain ends Dissolution with France.

1670 A rebellion of Ukrainian Cossacks (in Polish territory) is crushed by Jan Sobiéski, using New Model Army tactics – heavy, disciplined squadrons working in turning blocks, defeating brilliant individual horsemen.

1672 British naval attacks and French invasion against the Netherlands. The Dutch fleet holds its own against the British in the Battle of Southwold Bay. William of Orange drives back the French army approaching Amsterdam by opening the Dutch sluices. The use of floodwater as a weapon becomes part of military strategy.

"There is one certain means by which I can be sure never to see my country's ruin... I will die in the last ditch"

William of Orange

1674 Jan Sobiéski enhances his reputation by crushing a strong Turkish army at Khorzim. He is soon elected as Jan III, king of Poland.

1683 The Turks lay siege to Vienna. They are driven back by the combined armies of Charles, duke of Lorraine and King Jan III of Poland.

1685 The last pitched battle on English soil, at Sedgemore, Somerset.

1686 Roman Catholics are readmitted to the English Army.

1687 James II receives papal nuncio.

1688

'The Glorious Revolution': William of Orange, grandson of Charles I, and his wife Mary, daughter of James II, land at Torbay with an army of 15,000 men. They are soon declared king and queen by both English and Scottish conventions. James II runs away to France and, with papal funding, he goes to Ireland to stir up Catholic anger.

1690 William III defeats his father-in-law (James II) in the Battle of the Boyne.

1692 The French fleet is destroyed by English fire ships at La Hague, ending plans for an invasion.

1694 French ships and harbours are bombarded by the English fleet at Dieppe, Le Havre and Dunkirk.

1698 An attempted palace coup at the Kremlin by the Streltzy, the czar's praetorian guard. Peter the Great has all the officers executed with maximum cruelty. Leopold of Anhalt-Dessau introduces goose-stepping into Prussian army drill.

1700
Charles XII of Sweden defeats the serf army of Peter the Great at the Battle of Narva. Swedes, armed with longer-range muskets packed with new iron ramrods, move on to take Warsaw and Krakow.

1702 William III dies; Queen Anne succeeds him. Protestant succession is assured to the House of Hanover.

The duke of Marlborough becomes captain-general of English armed forces.

1703 The Swedes defeat the Russians at Rultusk.

1704 The War of the Spanish Succession. After a brilliantly organized march to the Danube, Marlborough joins forces with Prince Eugene of Savoy to defeat the French at Donauworth and a larger French and Bavarian army in a costly victory, with much wastage of infantry, at the Battle of Blenheim. The Royal Navy takes Gibraltar.

1705 The Royal Navy takes Barcelona.

1706 Marlborough conquers the Spanish Netherlands, exposing the military pretensions of Louis XIV with a shattering and deadly assault on tightly packed French infantry at Ramillies. Prince Eugene moves south to take Turin.

1707 Union between England and Scotland creates 'Great Britain'.

1708 Marlborough and Eugene again combine to defeat Vendôme's attempt to recover Flanders, with a devastating victory at Oudenarde.

Charles of Sweden, with Cossack allies, invades the Ukraine.

1709

Peter the Great defeats the Swedes at the Battle of Poltava. Marlborough becomes known as 'the Butcher', after the death of many French prisoners of war after Oudenarde. The same happens when he takes Tournai, and he is called the same by his own men, when he wins in 'the bloodiest bog' of Malplaquet.

1711 John Churchill, duke of Marlborough, is dismissed as commander-in-chief .

1713 The Treaty of Utrecht is signed. Spain cedes Gibraltar and Minorca to Britain.

1714 The death of Queen Anne. When her successor, George Louis, elector of Hanover, is crowned as King George I, his first order is the reinstatement of Marlborough.

1715 The Jacobite rebellion in Scotland, 'the Fifteen', led by the earl of Mar, with the object of restoring the Stuart line, is suppressed at battles at Sheriffmuir and Preston.

1717 Marlborough's old comrade-in-arms, Prince Eugene of Savoy, disperses a Turkish expeditionary army near Belgrade.

1722 Marlborough dies while examining a new Swiss weapon – a rifle.

1723 Prussia establishes the first full-time bureaucracy as a Ministry for War.

1727 The Spanish besiege Gibraltar. The British army recruits Hessian mercenaries after the death of George I (succeeded by his son, George II, who reigns until 1760).

1728 Spain raises the siege of Gibraltar after 14 months. The Treaty of Seville establishes 'understanding' between Britain and Spain, and is also recognized by French emissaries.

1739 Persians, under Nadir Shah, attack into India – Delhi is sacked.

1740 The First Silesian War – Frederick of Prussia invades territory of the new Empress Maria Theresa of Austria (and, soon, of Hungary).

1741 Prussia conquers Silesia: Brieg, Neissa, Glatz and Olmütz become the first prizes to bring Frederick II the addition 'Great'. Britain mediates a truce between Prussia and Austria.

1742 The truce is immediately broken. The Prussian army withdraws from Olmütz, as agreed. It then swings north, attacks a bivouacked Austrian army in the rear, near Chotusitz, and annihilates them. The Prussian Ministry for War notates this as a 'rehearsal'. The Peace of Berlin ends the First Silesian war: the Prussians demands are all acceded to, so that Maria Theresa's coronation should not be postponed.

1743
British artillery defeats the French at the Battle of Dettingen, using a new ballistic pendulum. This gives gunners the ability to measure the power of a given quantity of gunpowder.

1744 The Second Silesian War: Frederick the Great takes Prague but is stalled by Austro-Saxon joint armies in Saxony itself.

1745 The British are defeated by French Maréchal de Saxe, at Fontenoy. Having promised to support Maria Theresa with both troops and money, the British renege and limp home to face the Scottish army led by Charles Edward Stuart, the 'Young Pretender'. 'Bonnie Prince Charlie' wins a narrow victory at Prestonpans and advances south towards Derby, where the Highlanders meet the veterans of Dettingen and are forced to retreat beyond Hadrian's Wall.

1746 The Scots rally at Falkirk and defeat a Hanoverian force unequipped with artillery. At Culloden, brand new cannons destroy the Scottish army. English and German foundries can cast cannon barrels as solid pieces and bore them out. This made cannons more accurate.

1751 Britain joins an Austro-Russian alliance against Prussia.

1752 British armed forces adopt the Gregorian calendar on 2 September. The next day becomes 14 September.

1755 French and British armies clash in North America. It is a clear French victory at Fort Duquesne (modern Pittsburgh).

1756 Perfidious Albion makes peace with Prussia. The Treaty of Westminster guarantees that both countries will declare war on France. Natives are restless in most British colonies: the French drive British presence from the Great Lakes with the help of Native American allies in canoes. In India, 120 British soldiers are imprisoned and die in 'the Black Hole of Calcutta'. Robert Clive sets out from Calcutta to attack the Nawab of Bengal, who is holding English fugitives at Fulta.

The Seven Years War begins in Bohemia with the Battle of Lobosik. The Saxon army breaks at Pirna and capitulates to Frederick the Great.

THE BLACK HOLE OF CALCUTTA
1756

The black hole of Calcutta was the name given to a notorious dungeon in Fort William, where the Nawab of Bengal, Siraj ud-Daulah is said to have held British prisoners of war following the capture of Fort William on 20 June, 1756. According to legend, conditions in the dungeon were so awful, and so cramped, that a large number of the men held there died from suffocation, crushing or heat exhaustion. John Zephaniah Holwell, a temporary governor of Bengal and head civil servant at the East India Company, once claimed that 123 prisoners out of 146, died during their incarceration in the black hole, though this claim has often been disputed as propaganda.

According to Holwell, the dungeon was a strongly barred room, which was not intended for the incarceration of more than two or three people at a time. The cell became so full that it was difficult for guards to close the door properly. Some prisoners attempted to bribe guards to move them to a larger room, but they refused because the Nawab was asleep, and nobody dared wake him. By nine o'clock that evening, several of the prisoners had died, and many more had become delirious. The crowd began crying out for water, and eventually one of the more sympathetic guards appeared at the bars with some. Holwell and two or three other prisoners took the water in their hats and, having had a sip, passed it back into the cell. Tragically, crowd began to clamour for the water, and in the commotion much of it was spilt. Then the prisoners lost control, and a fearful tumult ensued, during which many of the weakest men were crushed to death under foot. Holwell's account of this terrifying night ends at eight o' clock the next morning, when the guards finally opened the doors of the cell. By that time the majority of the prisoners had died, and the men who were still alive sat stupefied by the heat combined with the horrific scenes they had witnessed. Holwell's account states that the dead were simply thrown into a ditch, Holwell and three other prisoners were transported to Murshidabad, and the remaining survivors were liberated when Major General Robert Clive, 1st Baron Clive of Plassey,arrived to rescue them.

1757 Clive retakes Calcutta.

Prussians defeat Austrians near Prague, then twice more at Rossbach and Leuthen. Frederick is not a great general: he is outwitted and defeated at Kolin by a determined Austrian cavalry, under Laudon.

1758 The same cavalry pressures a Prussian force to retreat into the small town of Neisse. In an attempt to relieve them, Frederick the Great is badly beaten at Hochkirch.

Two junior colonial officers retake Fort Duquesne from the French. Their names are Majors Forbes and Washington.

Clive's Bengal Lancers force Dutch capitulation at Chinswa: Clive becomes governor of Bengal.

1759 The Austrian general, Laudon, again outmanoeuvres Frederick the Great at Kunersdorf.

The British gain Quebec from the French and James Wolfe defeats Louis Joseph Montcalm on the Heights of Abraham – both generals are killed in action. Both are revered by their men and memorialized by them, in statues. A strict triple code is developed for heroic equestrian statuary of generals: (i) if both the horse's front feet are on the ground, the 'hero' died in battle; (ii) if one foot is raised, he died of wounds received in battle; (iii) if both feet are up – reared, in a little irony perhaps – the general died in bed.

1760 Austrians defeat the Prussians, again, at Landshut and take Glatz, but are horribly beaten at Torgau, then again in a huge battle at Liegnitz, on the same field and river bends where Ogodei of the Mongols crushed the papal and Teutonic knights in 1241.

1762 The Royal Navy ranges worldwide: Marines seize Manila, Martinique, Grenada and Havana.

1763
The 'Peace of Paris' ends the seven years war.

> ***"Our superiority in this war (Seven Years War) rendered our regard for this people (Native Americans) still less, which had always been too little... Decorums, which are necessary at least in dealing with barbarous as with civilized nations, were neglected"***

The Annual Register, or a View of the History, Politics and Literature for the year 1763.

1763 India and Indians trouble the British army: Hyder Ali conquers Kanara, Mysore, and a combination of Indian tribes rise near Detroit – their raids spread rapidly east.

1767 The Burmese invade Siam.

The New York Assembly is suspended when it refuses to support or provide quartering for troops.

1768 Boston also refuses to quarter 'British' troops. Gurkhas conquer Nepal.

1770 Five civilians die during the 'Boston Massacre', a brawl between Bostonian civilians and British troops.

1771 Russia completes its conquest of the Crimea and reaches agreement with the Prussians about partition of Poland.

1772 The Boston Assembly threatens secession.

1773
The Boston Tea Party.

> **“ The distinctions between Virginians, Pennsylvanians, New Yorkers, and New Englanders are no more. I Am Not A Virginian, But An American! ”**

Patrick Henry in 1774, following the Boston Tea Party.

1775 Peasants' revolts in Bohemia against serfdom.

Rich American slave-owners murder British soldiers at Lexington and Fort Ticonderoga. British troops rally and disperse gunmen at Bunker Hill; they also repulse an attack on Quebec led by one Benedict Arnold.

Unwilling to set brother against brother, the British government hires 29,000 German mercenaries for war in the American colonies.

1776
George Washington defeats Hessian troops at Trenton (pictured). *Benedict Arnold* is sunk on Lake Champlain.

1777 Americans import French troops under Lafayette to fight for them, and a German general, Baron Frederic Augustus von Steuben, to organise the army.

1778 Washington signs treaties with both France and Holland; rejects British peace offers; ignores Native American risings in Cherry Valley, New York and Wyoming Valley, Pennsylvania, and welcomes French warships into Delaware Bay. Meanwhile, Britain has more serious military concerns in Senegal, in Grenada, with the Mahrattas in India and with the war of the Bavarian Succession.

1779 Spain takes advantage of American pressure to declare war on Britain and again besieges Gibraltar.

The US Congress dispatches cavalry to the Wyoming Valley to massacre rebellious Native Americans.

THE GREAT SIEGE OF GIBRALTAR
1779

The great siege of Gibraltar was an attempt by the Spanish and the French to take Gibraltar from the British during the American War of Independence. Gibraltar was crucial to the British because it was a key link in the nation's control of the sea. If Britain lost it, the strength and status of the British Navy (which was generally regarded as the best in the world) would be left in doubt. The British forces in Gibraltar were led by George Augustus Elliot, an inspirational and extremely experienced military man who had already served in the Austrian war of Succession and the British expedition against Cuba.

Spanish and French naval fleets entered the bay of Gibraltar in July 1779, and an enormous army simultaneously built fortresses, redoubts and entrenchments from which to attack the garrison from solid ground. As time went on bread became almost impossible to get, and availability was restricted to children and the sick. Small rations of salt meat and biscuits became the troops daily diet, along with an occasional supplement of four ounces of rice. Despite these terrible hardships morale stayed generally high. Most historians attribute this to the brilliant leadership skills of George Augustus Elliot.

In January 1780, British Admiral Sir George Rodney was successful in driving off the French and Spanish fleets for long enough to allow supply ships and extra troops to reach the harbour, and another major resupply took place in 1781. Occasionally a small ship found the strength and the courage it needed to run the blockade – in order to supply the besieged British with vital aid and food, but starvation was always close at hand, and the siege dragged on for over three years. Throughout this period there were regular exchanges of artillery, presided over by a corps of sharpshooters led by Lieutenant Burleigh of the 39th Regiment.

On 13 September 1782, the French and Spanish, who were fed up with trying to starve the British out of Gibraltar, finally launched a major attack. Their offensive included approximately 100,000 men, 48 ships and 450 cannons. By this time most of the houses had been destroyed, the majority high buildings and high towers had been pulled down, and the streets were unpaved and un-passable. A total of 200 heavy guns open-fired from floating batteries in the bay, and a further 400 guns fired on the garrison from the fortresses on the land side. During the ensuing battle, the British were successful in destroying almost the entire enemy fleet, and killing almost 5,000 men on board the ships. The siege continued for some months after the battle, but eventually, after three years and seven months, the French and Spanish retreated. The British were left battered and bruised with losses of 1,231 men, and 8,000 expanded barrels of gunpowder, but they retained control of Gibraltar. Ownership of the rock is still a controversial issue between the Spanish and the British governments, though Spain now pursues its case through more diplomatic channels.

1780 French troops take Newport, Rhode Island and Benedict Arnold tries to surrender West Point.

Serfdom is abolished in both Bohemia and Hungary.

1781 British forces cease land operations in America after a defeat at Yorktown; the last troops withdraw from Savannah and Charleston.

1782 Benjamin Franklin presses American advantage in Paris peace talks. The British are too busy to negotiate. India is ablaze, with a rising by Tippo Sahib in Mysore, plus the Mahratta war and the Treaty of Salbai. By sea, Admiral Howe is able to relieve the siege of Gibraltar.

1783 The Peace of Versailles.

1784 Peace treaty agreed with Tippo Sahib, in Mysore; its terms hold throughout the Raj. And Benjamin Franklin returns triumphantly from Paris.

1789 The French Revolution. Bastille prison is stormed; Lafayette (returned from America) becomes commander of the National Guard.

The Storming of the Bastille
1789

At 3.30 am on the 14 July 1789 a huge, furious mob marched to the fortress of the Bastille in Paris, searching for gunpowder and prisoners that had been taken by King Louis XVI – the detested monarch. The defenders were prepared. They had installed twelve more guns on the walls between the towers, each capable of launching 24-ounce case shots at anyone who dared attack the gargantuan fortress. The governor, Marquis de Launay, had also drafted in 32 Swiss soldiers, led by Lieutenant Deflue, to help defend the Bastille's thick rock walls. However, the Marquis had seriously underestimated the feelings of ordinary French people in the Parisian commune at this time. The defenders expected approximately 100 angry subjects to launch an attack, but there were 300 hungry and furious men and women ready to give their lives in protest against the over-taxing and overbearing French establishment that night. That group included some members of the newly formed National Guard, who had left their posts in order to protest.The besiegers penetrated the fortress easily, breaking through the arsenal and into the first courtyard before cutting the drawbridge, and storming through the wooden door behind it. Next, the mob demanded that the bridge be let down. De Launay issued an ultimatum to a ring-leader named Hulin: He claimed he had 20,000 pounds of gunpowder in his possession, and if the mob did not allow him and his men to leave peacefully, he would gladly blow the entire Bastille sky-high, as well as everyone in it. The crowd's leaders refused to negotiate, and the bridges were finally lowered on De Launay's command. He and his men were captured by the mob, and dragged out of the Bastille into the filthy streets of Paris. The rioters paraded through the streets, showing off their captives and cutting off many heads. A revolt had become a revolution.

1790 Benjamin Franklin dies. The Austrian army enters Brussels and crushes Belgian demands for independence.

1792 Revolutionary France declares war on Austria, Prussia and Sardinia. The Austrian/Prussian invading force is stopped at the Battle of Valmy. French troops cross the Rhine, take Brussels and drive the Austrians from the Netherlands.

1793 Louis XVI is executed. The Holy Roman Empire declares war on France. The USA proclaims its neutrality.

1794 The US navy is founded.

1795 Napoleon Bonaparte is appointed commander of the French revolutionary army in Italy. The French occupy Luxembourg, Mannheim and Belgium. Austria signs an armistice.

1796 Napoleon knows that the Austrians armisticed with a forked tongue, he brings two Austrian armies to battle at Lodi and Arcol, and defeats both.

Britain seizes the Isle of Elba.

1797
Napoleon defeats the Austrians at Rivoli, takes Mantua and advances through the Tirol to Vienna. He is appointed to command revolutionary forces for the invasion of England, though he himself recognizes the supremacy of the Royal Navy. Admiral Jervis and a Captain Nelson defeat the Spanish fleet off Cape St Vincent. British naval power is threatened by mutinies at the Nore and Spithead.

1798 The French capture Rome and proclaim a new Roman republic. Pope Pius VI escapes.

Malta is seized by the French on their way to Alexandria. Napoleon wins the 'Battle of the Pyramids' and becomes master of Egypt. Unable to match French power on land, a Royal Navy squadron, led by Horatio Nelson, attacks and burns the French fleet in Aboukir Bay, west of the Rosetta mouth of the River Nile.

1799 Napoleon advances into Syria and besieges Acre. He then returns to France, overthrows the directory government and becomes consul.

1800 Napoleon's generals defeat a Turkish army at Heliopolis and advance on Cairo. The revolutionary army also triumphs triply over the Austrians at Biberach, Höchstadt and Hohenlinden, and approaches Vienna. The revolutionaries also make a remarkable crossing of the St Bernard Pass in the Alps, to crush the Austrians at Marenga.

1801 The Peace of Lunéville between Austria and France marks the formal end of the Holy Roman Empire.

Nelson defeats Danish and French fleets off Copenhagen.

1802 The Peace of Amiens – Britain and the French republic take a break from hostilities.

Meanwhile, war technology continues to advance: the British develop cylinder-burned charcoal, and the first practical paddle steamer is built.

1803 The first use of the exploding canister shell, invented by Henry Shrapnel, terrifies and subdues the Sindhia of Gwalior in the second Mahratta war. Arthur Wellesley, the British commander in India, is very impressed.

1804 Napoleon is crowned emperor in Paris – by his own hands. Pope Pius VII, who was supposed to perform the coronation, is left on the bench in Notre Dame Cathedral. General Jean Bernadotte, the victor of Marengo, becomes marshall of France.

1805
The Battles of Ulm and Austerlitz break Austria's armies and severely damage Russia's. Austria sues Napoleon for peace.

Only at sea could Napoleon be challenged. Sir John Jervis, the victor at St Vincent, now said of the French army's mastery of Europe, and of Napoleon's clear intention to invade England: 'I do not say he cannot come. I merely say that he cannot come by sea.'

The Battle of Trafalgar
1805

The Battle of Trafalgar was fought on 21 October, 1805, in the sea off Cape Trafalgar on the Spanish Coast. It was here that Nelson struck the decisive British blow of the entire war. His victory in the battle of Trafalgar has come to represent the end of Napoleon's plans to invade England, and it also helped to further secure the British Navy's reputation as 'ruler of the waves' throughout the next century. The French and Spanish fleets, led by Admiral Vileneuve, had more ships than the British: a total of 33 ships of the line, compared to Nelson's 27. In addition, the combined fleet had more guns per ship than their counterparts. However, the Royal Navy were much better drilled, and could fire their guns at least three times for every two French or Spanish shots. The battle itself went largely according to Nelson's plan. At the beginning, the combined fleet approached in a ragged curved line heading north, the British fleet approached in two fairly neat columns. The winds were light that day, and the ships moved very slowly. Most of the combat at the battle of Trafalgar happened at very close range, with ships firing at their enemies from only a few yards away. The guns on board these warships fired heavy cannon balls and chain linked shot designed to wreck rigging, but they also tore through limbs, and did huge damage to human cargo on board. The British cut the combined fleet's line of battle, destroying or capturing almost all the French and Spanish ships. The British retained all its ships, but lost the greatest naval commander in its history. Admiral Nelson was shot by an enemy marksman on the deck of his ship HMS *Victory*, and perished soon after victory had been declared. He had succeeded in saving his nation. Before battle commenced, Nelson had declared himself confident of two things, firstly that the British fleet would be victorious, and secondly, that he would die during the battle. Nelson was proven right on both counts.

1806 The Royal Navy mounts the longest sea blockades in history, with hundreds of ships continuously at sea off the French coast and elsewhere.

Napoleon defeats the Prussians at Jena and Auerstädt and occupies Berlin, where he declares the Continental System, which essentially closes all the ports of Europe to British shipping.

The French army, under Murat, deploys eastwards, moving on to seize Warsaw.

1807
The Battle of Eylau (pictured). Combined Prussian and Russian forces hold the French advance. In terrible conditions, much like the western front of the First World War, the generals call it a draw after 12 hours of pointless effort. Approximately 100,000 men have been killed. Weeks later, after a further French victory at Friedland forces access to the port and the many cannon of Königsberg, the true pointlessness of Eylau is consummately manifested in the Treaty of Tilsit, signed in person by the emperor of France, the czar of Russia and the king of Prussia, all of whom state they have no quarrel outstanding one with another. Prussia even agrees to emancipate its serfs, but the czar does not. Then they all return home, enabling Napoleon to turn his attention to Portugal, which his armies quickly occupy. The dethroned Portuguese royal family escapes to Brazil.

1808 Napoleon moves on through Spain, taking Madrid and Barcelona, both after brief but bloody sieges, and on to Italy, seizing both Rome and Naples. The new king of Naples, by popular acclaim, and at the age of just 41, is Joachim Murat.

> ***"Never interrupt your enemy when he is making a mistake"***

Napoleon Bonaparte.

1809 Britain still tries to grapple with the French Empire, anywhere where there is salt water nearby. Britain agrees to the 'Treaty of the Dardanelles', with Turkey, just in case Napoleon should pass that way. He does not. He returns to central Europe, secure in his Tilsit truce with Russia/Prussia and attacks Austria. He takes Vienna, brushes aside a setback at Aspern and forces the Habsburgs to the humiliating 'Peace of Schönbrunn', with a crushing victory at Wagram. Austria joins the Continental System, agreeing to close all its ports to British trade – this is not too onerous an undertaking for a landlocked country. The Swedes also hurry to agree with Napoleon: they elect Jean Bernadotte as crown prince.

In mid 1809 Napoleon annexes the Papal States. Britain gets a new foreign minister: his name is Wellesley, christened 'Richard'. His brother, Arthur, now lands a British army at Oporto, against stern French opposition. At last there are British boots on the ground fighting the French. General Wellesley tells his brother that he is moving inland. Portuguese troops support him and the French are defeated at Talavera. Richard Wellesley tells Arthur that he will be created first duke of Wellington.

A momentous year, 1809: Napoleon even finds time to divorce the Empress Josephine. And, in a log cabin, far away, Abraham Lincoln is born.

1810 The year of Napoleon's zenith. He marries Archduchess Marie Louise of Austria.

Napoleon now annexes Holland, Bremen, Hamburg, Lauenburg, Lübeck and Hanover. The Napoleonic acquisition of Hanover *really* irritates the British king, George III, a Hanoverian: his sanity begins to crumble.

1811 When Napoleon annexes Oldenburg, the madness of King George becomes public knowledge.

Austria goes bankrupt: her armies crumble.

Wellington defeats revolutionary armies at Fuentes de Oñoro and Albuera but, like Nelson, he cannot find a French force large enough to make such victories decisive in the Peninsular war.

1811
William Henry Harrison smashes with artillery a Native American group of horse-archers led by Chief Tecumseh at Tippecanoe, Indiana.

1812 Two German generals with the famous names of Scharnhorst and Gneisenau – later to become celebrated in the Kriegsmarine – resign when the Prussian government grants free passage to French troops en route to invade Russia.

Napoleon's first revolutionary army crosses the Niemen river, entering Russia on 24 June. They make the 'impossible' pontoon crossing of the Viliya river, thereby surprising and defeating a huge Russian army at Smolensk; then fighting a bloody but indecisive battle at Borodino in September. The emperor enters a deserted Moscow, but orders a retreat on 19 October, establishing a rearguard on both banks of the Berezina river. He leaves Murat in command and hurries back to Paris to counter a palace coup led by General Claude Malet, who is quickly executed.

Much the same happens to British Prime Minister Spencer Perceval in the House of Commons. The French launch a disastrous winter retreat from Russia, only 20,000 troops out of 550,000 survive. The USA invades Canada.

1813 Prussia declares war on a bleeding, disorganized and frostbitten France. Combined Russo-Prussian forces expel French troops from Dresden. They march to join Napoleon's army at Lützen, where the emperor is once again victorious. Cavalry under Prussian General Blücher pin the French force against and then into the River Katzbach, at Wahlstatt. Napoleon responds by bloodily retaking Dresden.

THE BATTLE OF NATIONS
1813

Napoleon's defeat at the Battle of Leipzig, which took place in Leipzig, Germany between 16-19 October, 1813, became one of the most crucial battles of the Napoleonic wars because it finally loosened his grip on central Europe. It has since been called the Battle of Nations, because of the sheer number of troops involved – over 500,000 soldiers - an exceptionally large number for any pitched battle. This made it the biggest battle of its kind in world history, up until the advent of the First World War. The anti-French forces of Russia, Austria, Prussia, Sweden, Britain, Spain, Portugal and some smaller German states had combined to form the sixth coalition. Napoleon's forces also happened to contain Germans, mostly representatives of the Rhine. The French and their allies numbered approximately 200,000 troops, whereas the forces of the sixth coalition are said to have numbered approximately 400,000. About half the world's cannons were there: around 700 French versus 1,500 for the coalition forces.

On day 1, Austrian General Schwatzenberg attacked in the south: Napoleon's counterattack rolled the Austrians and Poles back to where they started. Marshall Blücher's forces stormed the city positions held by Marshall Marmont: the Prussians and Sileians were repelled.

Day 2 was almost a rest day, but the Swedish army arrived and deployed to the north-east, under the command of Jean-Baptiste Bernadotte.

On day 3, 18 October, the French were attacked on all sides by over 350,000 troops. They held their lines for 9.5 hours. Napoleon withdrew nearly 100,000 men over a single-span bridge across the river Elster. He always claimed that in another hour he would have brought out 20,000 more, if explosive charges on the bridge had not detonated prematurely. The French Empire left over 80,000 men behind at Leipzig: 46,000 killed plus 21,000 wounded or sick; 15,000 Frenchmen were captured, as were 325 cannons. Napoleon retreated eventually to the west bank of the Rhine. The French adventure to the east was over.

Wellington's victory at Vitoria enables him to seize San Sebastian and cross the Pyrenees. As he enters France, Blücher seizes two bridges and brings a Prussian army across the Rhine, also reaching French soil before Christmas.

Elsewhere, the US army takes York (now Toronto); they are then soundly beaten by a scratch British/Canadian force at Chrysler's Farm, near Montreal. In response, the Americans burn Newark, aka Niagara-on-the-Lake, before being ejected from Fort Niagara and then driven back beyond Buffalo, to which the British and Canadians set fire before returning across the border. In one of the mightiest single-ship battles of the age of fighting sail, HMS *Shannon* not only defeats, but captures the US frigate *Chesapeake*, a victory greeted by the Royal Navy as 'the best news since Trafalgar'.

1814
Murat (pictured) deserts Napoleon and joins the allied forces. His tactical betrayals contribute to crushing French defeats at La Rothière, Bar-sur-Aube and Laon. Allied armies enter Paris on 30 March. Wellington wryly approves a victory parade on April Fools' Day. Murat is asked, as the French Empire is collapsing, if he has calculated on any desertions from Bonaparte's army: 'Not upon a man, from the colonel to the private in a regiment – both inclusive,'he replied. 'We may pick up a Marshall or two, perhaps – but no one worth a damn.'

1814 Napoleon abdicates and is banished to Elba. He leaves Paris on 11 April, the day before Louis XVIII turns up to claim the French throne as his 'hereditary right'.

Meanwhile, white colonialists in America defeat a British force at Chippewa and capture a Canadian flotilla on Lake Champlain. A British force then burns the new capital, Washington. This war is officially ended by the Treaty of Ghent (however, no one is able to inform the combatants, who continue fighting).

1815 Specifically excluded from all negotiations at Ghent is the entire, largely French, territory of Louisiana. The Royal Navy deploys about 1,600 British soldiers and marines some 15 km (9.5 miles) south of New Orleans at the time the treaty is signed. An American major-general named Andrew Jackson, attacks, with overwhelming force, the small British presence in what was still, unarguably, crown territory. Over the next week, the British hold their ground against a massive artillery barrage. By 8 January, despite the partial failure of attempts at reinforcement from the ships anchored offshore, and having exhausted their ammunition, the British troops still repulse two assaults by Jackson's army. When General John Lambert orders them to withdraw, the British have taken 2,037 casualties; the American dead number 13. The US victory helps to propel Jackson into the White House.

Meanwhile, in Vienna, there is a fairly hurried closure, lasting about one hundred days. Napoleon leaves Elba and lands in the south of France. Louis XVIII sends an army under Marshall Ney to swat the few hundred imperial storm troopers who surround their emperor. Ney delivers his army into Napoleon's command. Louis escapes to England.

Metternich draws up a new alliance, binding together Austria, Russia, Britain and Prussia.

The Battle of Waterloo: Napoleon issues a new liberal constitution, *Le Champs de Mar* – May Fields – and takes 74,000 troops into the field on 18 June at Waterloo, near Brussels. He is opposed by Wellington, with 24,000 British infantry, supported by Belgian and Dutch infantry, plus cavalry and artillery to around the same number – a total of some 47,000 men. What is absent when Napoleon orders the assault is the rest of Metternich's coalition: no Austrian troops, no Russians, and 20,000 missing Prussians. Led by Marshall Gebhard von Blücher, they are separated from the main battlefield by monsoon rains and miles of deep Flanders mud. Wellington says to his officers of the initial carriage: 'Hard pounding this, gentlemen; let's see who will pound longest.' It soon becomes clear: the French would. Wellington's infantry loses half its men: the Dutch and Belgians more – a total of almost 26,000 casualties. As Napoleon's victory ground closer, the Prussians finally arrived. After the battle, Wellington reported: 'It has been a damned serious business – Blücher and I have lost 30,000 men. It has been a damned nice thing – the nearest run thing you ever saw in your life ... By God! I don't think it would have been done if I had not been there.' Wellington's casualty figure was underestimated: both sides took closer to 40,000 casualties each.

Four days later, Napoleon abdicated for the second time. He was sent into perpetual exile in the deep South Atlantic Ocean, on the remote island of St Helena. King Louis sidled back into Versailles in time to sign the second Peace of Paris. He immediately ordered the execution of Michel Ney, for his aid to his emperor. And the king of Naples, AKA Joachim Murat, was court-martialled, and shot.

1818 As the allies of Waterloo withdrew their final troops from France, Jean Bernadotte, caitiff-martial, was crowned king of Sweden, as Charles XIV, instigating over 190 years of Swedish neutrality.

1820 The first iron steamship, *Aaron Manby*, is built in London. By sailing to Paris via the Thames, Manche and Seine, she makes the first seagoing passage by an iron ship.

1821 The death of Napoleon, aged 52. His last words are reputed to be either *'Tête d'Armée'* or *'France, l'Armée, Joséphine'*. Both army references may be subsumed in his writing of war itself: *'A la guerre, les trios quarts sont des affaires morales, la balance des forces réelles n'est que pour un autre quart'* ('In war, moral considerations make up three-quarters of the matter: the relative balance of manpower accounts only for the remaining quarter'). And in the ultimate recognition about all warfare after the deadly retreat from Moscow in 1812: *'Du sublime au ridicule il n'ya a qu'un pas'* ('there is only one step from the sublime to the ridiculous').

Another Frenchman makes his contribution: Henri-Joseph Paixhans invents the explosive shell, causing Victor Hugo to write: *'Terre! L'obus est Dieu, y Paixhans son prophète'* ('Earth! The shell is God, and Paixhans is his prophet').

On another continent, Simon Bolivar defeats the Spanish army of occupation at Carabobo, and ensures the 'independence' of Venezuela. The aboriginal inhabitants, who had hoped that all the conquistadors would one day go home, are left disappointed.

1822 The Turkish fleet occupies the island of Chios and massacres its Greek inhabitants. In reprisal, Greeks set fire to the flagship of the Turkish admiral. The Turkish army then invades Greece.

1824 Simon Bolivar proclaims himself 'Emperor of Peru' after swatting some more Spanish infantry. Turkish ships seize the island of Ipsara, but their land forces are halted at Mitylene.

1825 Czar Nicholas I crushes the Decembrist revolt in Russia. Cossack cavalry is characteristically effective against civilians on foot.

1826 To distract both his archdukes and peasants, Nicholas I declares war on Persia.

1827 The Turkish army enters Athens. The Russian army occupies Erivan (Armenia).

1828 Russian ambitions grow: Nicholas declares war on Turkey, hoping to end the occupation of Aegean islands and mainland Greece.

1829 The Peace of Adrianople ends the Russo-Turkish war: Turkey acknowledges the independence of Hellenes. The development of a practical ship's screw – this will eventually replace paddle wheels.

1830 France invades and occupies Algeria. J N von Drayse invents the breech-loading needle-gun.

1831 The Polish Diet secedes from Russia. Czar Nicholas's Cossacks crush street revolts and a scratch Polish army is overwhelmed at the Battle of Ostroleka: the revolution collapses.

1832 Von Clausewitz's magnum opus *On War* is published, posthumously, by his widow. It is soon translated and celebrated as 'a treasure of the human spirit': the most influential western book on war ever written. He wrote: 'War is, above all, a question of character'.

1836
'Remember the Alamo'. Texas secedes from Mexico after heavy fighting between Sam Houston's irregulars (including frontiersmen like Davy Crockett and Jim Bowie, both killed in the Alamo fortress siege) and a Mexican army under Santa Ana.

1838 Battle of Blood River, in Natal. The Boers (Dutch farmer/settlers) defeat the Zulus, using rifles against iklwas (spears).

1839
The outbreak of the first Opium War between Britain and China (until 1842). It may be worth noting that British forces are fighting in favour of opium – it was the 'currency' with which British India paid for Chinese goods like porcelain, silk and tea. Britain gained Hong Kong and five 'treaty ports' in this war, forcing the Chinese to accept opium imports against their will.

1840 The British army 'subdues' resistance in Afghanistan.

1841 In one of the most effective single-ship strikes against the US navy, the USS *Creole*, carrying slaves from Virginia to Louisiana, is seized by the slaves and sails into the British port of Nassau, where they become free.

1843 Maori wars against the British occupation of New Zealand.

The French extend their North African colonies with brutal use of force in both Algeria and Morocco. The Treaty of Tangier ends some of the killing.

1846 After failing to agree a price for the purchase of the 'New Mexico' territories from old Mexico, the US army takes them anyway, defeating a small Mexican force at Palo Alto before getting around to a formal declaration of war. The US army then invades in strength, occupies Sante Fe in August and declares annexation of all New Mexico.

Gun cotton is invented in Basle, Switzerland.

1847 The Mexican–US war continues. The US army enters Mexico City.

1848 The Treaty of Guadeloupe Hidalgo ends the Mexican–US war. The US gets Texas, New Mexico, California, Utah, Nevada, Arizona and parts of Colorado and Wyoming.

Widespread civil unrest in Europe. Some armed forces are unable, or unwilling, to fire on their own citizens in Paris, Vienna, Milan, Venice, Prague, Berlin, Rome and Budapest. Metternich resigns. Louis Napoleon is elected president of the French republic. Sardinia declares war on Austria in the chaos, attempting to annexe Venice: their soldiers briefly hold the Grand Canal, then are crushed at Custozza. They take the long sea route home.

1849 Claude E Minie invents the Minie-ball, an improved muzzle-loading rifle-bullet. It is the preferred ammunition of most protagonists in both the Crimean and American civil wars.

1850 Taiping rebellion in China. Hung Hiu-Tsuen proclaims himself emperor, attacks Peking, and takes both Nanking and Shanghai. Wilhelm Bauer builds the first hand-powered submarine. It is tiny and primitive, but it will submerge and surface.

The First Submarine
1850

The submarine existed, in sketch form at least, in the days of Leonardo Da Vinci, but it was not until 1850 that Wilhelm Bauer, a German inventor and engineer, invented and built the first hand-powered version. Bauer's father was a sergeant in the Bavarian Cavalry, so Wilhelm, having completed a woodturning apprenticeship, followed in his father's footsteps and joined the military as an artillery engineer. During the German/Danish war for Schleswig-Holstien, the German army found that they needed a ship that could get past blockades. In order to accomplish this, Bauer began studying hydraulics and ship construction. However, before he could finalize his design, Germany pulled out of the dispute, surrendering Schleswig-Holstien to the Danish. Bauer was determined to bring his work to some kind of resolution, and so he deserted the German army in favour of the forces of Schleswig-Holstien, where he was free to continue his project. Bauer was of very low military rank, and he faced a myriad of problems finding the funding he needed. He finally succeeded with the help of another German inventor and industrialist Ernst Werner von Siemens, whose company is now one of the most successful electro-technology companies in the world. Their first model, a prototype Brandtaucher, was designed as a diving incendiary ship. It would dive under a vessel, fix an electronically triggered mine to its hull before escaping and igniting the mine from a safe distance. Following trials, Bauer was granted the funds to build a full-scale version of the Brandtaucher, but first the military insisted he make some money-saving changes to the way it worked. The first full scale Brandtaucher was 28 ft (8.5 m) long and weighed 70,000 lb (31,751 kg). No suitable mechanical-powered system existed at this time, and so the submarine was driven by two sailors who used their hands and feet to turn an enormous treadmill. The third member of the crew, the captain, was positioned at the stern, and his responsibility was to operate the rudders and other controls.

Bauer's original design for the Brandtaucher meant that the vessel achieved submersion when a number of water tanks became filled with seawater. The cost reducing changes meant that, instead, part of the submarine itself became flooded when the submarine dived, rendering the vessel dangerously unstable. The thickness of the hull and the dimensions of the pumps had also been reduced during the military's penny-pinching exercise.

Initial trials for the full scale Brandtaucher took place in December 1850. Following these, Bauer wanted to make several important changes, but his superiors insisted on a public demonstration on 1 February 1851. It almost ended in disaster. As the Brandtaucher reached a depth of around 30ft (9.14 m), the thin walls began to crack under the pressure. The pumps were also overwhelmed, the propeller wheel was damaged and the vessel began to keel over. Slowly the submarine sank to the bottom of Kiel harbour, where Bauer and his crew waited for six hours before they were able to free themselves from the craft. The sunken submarine was finally raised in 1887, and can now be seen as an exhibit at the museum of Military History in Dresden.

1851 Ordnance factories develop methods for measuring pressure inside the barrels and breeches of cannons, making possible much more effective ballistic potential – the range and weight of the projectile is greatly increased.

THE MODERN ERA

1852–1945

1852 The British army begins using the Enfield rifle – a more accurate, longer range and heavier bullet (Minie-ball type).

1853 Czar Nicholas I orders Russian forces to occupy Turkish possessions among Danubian principalities. Turkey declares war on Russia and attacks Russian warships off Sinope. The Russian navy destroys almost the entire Turkish fleet: the Crimean War then begins.

1854 Britain and France form an alliance with Turkey and declare war on Russia. There are unopposed landings in Crimea. Sebastopol is besieged. Russians are defeated at Balaklava and Inkerman. Turkey agrees to Austrian occupation of Danubian principalities until the end of the war – Austrian troops eject the Russian occupying forces. During the Crimean War, the Russian navy makes the first use of mines as strategic weapons.

1855 The death of Czar Nicholas. Russian defenders capitulate at Sebastopol – the French and British occupy the port and city.

1856
Queen Victoria institutes Britain's highest military award for gallantry – the Victoria Cross. The medals are manufactured from metal melted down from Russian cannon captured in the Crimea.

British warships bombard Canton – gunboat diplomacy – to cow the natives into following British trade requirements.

1857 Indian mutiny against British rule. Siege of Delhi, then surrender and occupation. British troops also fight their way into Cawnpore and kill many mutineers.

The Royal Navy destroys the Chinese fleet, and brings relief column to Lucknow. British and French soldiers occupy Canton.

1858 The Treaty of Tientsin ends the Anglo-Chinese war. Similarly, but even more unilaterally, the British Raj proclaims peace throughout India.

1859 France launches *La Gloire*, the first seagoing armoured ship. Uninvolved in the land-based Franco-Austrian war, Austrian armies are heavily defeated at Magenta and Solferino.

1860 Civil war in Italy. Garibaldi and his thousand redshirts (*'i Mille'*) sail from Genoa, and take Marsala, Palermo and Naples. Victor

Emmanuel II, king of Sardinia, invades the Papal States, easily defeating, then converting, many of the pope's underpaid soldiers to his cause. Garibaldi proclaims Victor Emmanuel 'King of Italy'.

Du Picq writes *Battle Studies*, focusing on the behaviour of men in battle. The second Maori War in New Zealand. South Carolina arms its militia, and secedes from the US when Abraham Lincoln is elected as the 16th president.

1861 The Confederate States of America is formed at the Congress of Montgomery. South Carolina is joined by the slave-states of Georgia, Alabama, Mississippi, Florida and Louisiana. Confederates bombard and seize Fort Sumter, in Charleston, on 12 April – the start of the American Civil War, aka 'The War between the States'. Lincoln calls for militia to suppress the Confederacy. The first major battle at Bull Run: the Confederate States of America ('the South') forces defeat those of the Union ('the North').

The king of Naples surrenders his army to Garibaldi at Gaeta. Italy is proclaimed a kingdom, with Victor Emmanuel as king.

1862 Union forces capture various Confederate forts, plus Jacksonville and New Orleans, but are defeated again at the second battle of Bull Run.

The Gatling gun is patented.

Two ironclad warships fight for the first time at sea: the USS *Monitor* (Union navy) and the CSS *Virginia* fought a battle, declared a draw, off Hampton Roads. The *Virginia*, formerly the USN frigate *Merrimock*, is scuttled at her moorings in the Norfolk navy yard when Union naval personnel abandon it. The two ships fired shot, grape, canister, musket and rifle balls at each other for 4½ hours, killing dozens of sailors but 'doing no damage to the ships whatsoever', according to Captain Buchanan of the *Virginia*. Any wooden ship would have been chewed to pieces.

> ***" Almost a week ago [The British] discovered that their whole wooden navy was useless...These are great times... Man has mounted science, and is now to run away with [it]... Before many centuries more... science may have the existence of mankind in its power, and the human race commit suicide by blowing up the world "***

Henry Adams, March 1862. Wooden naval vessels were rendered obsolete by the invention of the ironclad warship.

1863 Heavy rifled cannons dominate the battlefields of the American Civil War. Made of high-quality cast-iron, they have three to six times the power of the guns at Waterloo. In the Union victories at Gettysburg and Vicksburg, hundreds of Confederate soldiers are killed by artillery before they come within sight of the Union lines. This is the first war also to witness large-scale use of railways, telegraph and breech-loading rifles.

1864 Danish forces are outnumbered and mauled by Austrian and Prussian invaders and forced to cede Schleswig-Holstein and Lauenburg to them.

Victor Emmanuel's Italy gives up its claim to Rome. Turin, then Florence, is named as capital.

Ulysses S Grant takes command of the Union armies, orders General Sherman to advance through Georgia, where he defeats the main body of the Confederate army in a bloody battle at Atlanta and proceeds to march to the sea at Savannah, destroying everything his army can reach on the way.

1865 The Union fleet takes Charleston, including Fort Sumter, where it all began. The Confederate capital, Richmond, surrenders to Ulysses S Grant. Robert E Lee, general-in-chief of the Confederate army, surrenders at Appomattox on 9 April. Five days later, President Lincoln is assassinated.

1866
The Seven Weeks War, provoked by Otto von Bismarck. The Austrian army is humiliated at the Battle of Königgrätz. Prussian expansion. Invasions and annexation of Hanover, Hesse, Nassau and Frankfurt, creating the first sense of 'Deutschland'. With Prussian support, Italy absorbs Venice. The Prussian army is now easily the most powerful in Europe, witnessing the triumphal use of dedicated and highly trained general staff.

1867 Garibaldi is taken prisoner during the Battle of Mentana, where French and papal troops interdict his 'March on Rome'.

Alfred Nobel invents dynamite.

1869 Conquest without war: following a Turkish ultimatum, Greek forces withdraw from Crete.

The Suez Canal is opened.

1870 Franco-Prussian War. France declares the war, but is not remotely ready to fight it. The supremacy of the Prussian army is absolute. At Weissenburg, Worth, Mars-la-Tour, Gravelotte and Sedan, the French army is easily dispatched. Napoleon III actually travels to Sedan to capitulate. Paris erupts with anger and refuses to surrender. Prussians besiege the city and resistance wanes.

1871
William I, king of Prussia, is proclaimed 'Emperor of Germany' at Versailles. Paris capitulates: the French National Assembly removes to Bordeaux. Armistice is formalized at the Peace of Frankfurt: France cedes Alsace-Lorraine and pays Prussia five billion francs to withdraw from the rest of the French territory it holds.

1871 Prussia is now so powerful it even wages cultural war – the persuasively anti-Catholic 'Kulturkampf' urges young Prussians to give their hearts and minds to their country, not to religion. That country is now 'Germany'. Bismarck becomes 'the Iron Chancellor', derived from his own self-description as 'a man of blood and iron'.

" War...must be recognized as an instinct of humanity, of divine origin, not to be replaced, as idealists hope, by any human device like tribunals of arbitration or submissive trust in the generosity of competitors "

O H Ernst *War*, 1877

1873 The last Prussian troops leave France.
1875 Alfred Nobel invents ballistite – smokeless gunpowder.
1876 Bulgaria, Serbia and Montenegro are all at war with Turkey.
1877 The Russians are also at war with Turkey. Their armies invade through Romania, cross the Danube and storm Kars. Another Russian force takes Plevna, in Bulgaria. Otto von Bismarck, chancellor of a united Germany, declines to use the might of Prussian arms to intervene.

1878 So Britain does. And, Britain chooses the wrong side. The Royal Navy dispatches a powerful fleet to Constantinople at the request of the Turkish sultan, borne on a wave of 'jingoism' from the British *canaille*. As Greece also declares war on Turkey, Britain resounds to the chant of: 'We don't want to fight, but by Jingo we will!' In the end, however, the Turks capitulate after a skirmish in the Shipka Pass. The Russians occupy Adrianople while they consider, then sign, an armistice.

> ***"Oh if the Queen were a man she would like to go and give those horrid Russians, whose word one cannot trust, such a beating"***

Queen Victoria to Benjamin Disraeli, January 1878

1879 Britain finds somebody else to fight – the Zulus.

THE ZULU IMPI
1879

The Zulu word 'impi' actually pertains to any group of armed men, but it is widely taken to mean 'regiment'. The Zulu word for regiment is actually 'ibutho'. For the purpose of this book, the former, most widely recognized meaning for 'impi' has been used.

The Zulu Impi's reputation for warfare dates back to the Battles of Isandhlwana and Rorke's Drift in Natal, South Africa. In the former conflict, the Impis outfought and out-thought British firepower during a solar eclipse. An entire battalion of the 24th Foot, the 1st Warwicks, of over 1,000 men, was slaughtered. The Zulus also acquired a thousand Martini-Henry rifles and all the 24th's ammunition: hundreds of thousands of Mimie-balls.

On 22 January, many of the same Impi, about 4,500 Zulu warriors, attacked Rorke's Drift, a small mission station defended by 139 men of the 2nd battalion: but not Englishmen, like the Warwicks. These were South Wales Borderers. What ensued was one of the most extraordinary actions of military history. At a cost of 17 killed, the Welshmen inflicted over 600 Zulu casualties and drove off the massed Impi. Eleven Victoria Crosses were awarded, the most for a single action before or since. There would have been more, but the Cross could not be awarded posthumously until 1905.

1880 Alfred Mahan publishes *The Influence of Seapower upon History, 1660–1783*. He advocates the command of the sea as a route to national greatness, referring as far back as the critical role played by Roman fleets during the Punic Wars and perorating with his hero, Admiral Nelson.

France sends its seapower to annexe Tahiti.

1881 Elsewhere, in South Africa, the Transvaal Boers repulse a British assault at Laing's Nek and defeat a strong British force at Majuba Hill: Britain recognizes, by the Treaty of Pretoria, the independent Transvaal republic.

1882 At the Hague Convention a three-mile limit for territorial waters is agreed. Steam-powered torpedo boats are being used for harbour defence. These evolved into the modern destroyer. Most maritime forces discard rigging and sails, for all except training ships.

1884 Mahdi rising in the Sudan: General C G Gordon is sent to Khartoum to negotiate. The Mahdi refuse to meet him and his forces occupy the colonial centre of Omdurman.

Germany joins the European imperial mania and becomes a colonial power in south-west Africa. Bismarck orders extensions into the Pacific.

1885
The Mahdi take Khartoum; General Gordon is killed in the assault. British forces retreat from the Sudan, also evacuating civilians. The Mahdi die from typhus.

1885 Germany annexes Tanganyika and Zanzibar. Prussian army assault tactics are used against African civilians. Faced with the German colonial threat, Britain dispatches armed forces to the Niger river, Bechuanaland, New Guinea and Port Hamilton, Korea.

1886 Brass cartridges for breech-loading cannons are developed.

1889 The first May Day celebrations are held in Paris. The Industrial Revolution, largely driven by war, had created a new labour versus employer consciousness. Among the celebrants of 1 May, as a day of awakening for the workers of the world, is another war-theorist and political philosopher, Friedrich Engels. As well as his socialist writings and his working relationship with Karl Marx, Engels wrote extensively about military history and ideas. He published numerous articles about army mobilisation and deployment. 'A concentrated army is a calamity,' he noted. 'It is a target; it cannot subsist, it cannot move, it can only fight.' He studied Prussian military texts, concluding that 'the deployment in width' of massed infantry by Frederick the Great could only be explained by the fact that the king personally was in command – 'members of royal families being notoriously feeble-minded'.

1891 During the Chilean revolutionary war, a self-propelled torpedo sinks an armoured warship for the first time.

1893 German General Staff conceive the 'Von Schlieffen Plan' for the final conquest of France, using a colossal right-wheel flanking movement through the Low Countries and then southwards, cutting off Paris from the sea.

1894
Japanese troops move into Seoul. Far from an attack, it is the prelude to a joint declaration by Japan and Korea of war against China. Port Arthur is attacked immediately: the Chinese are forced to retreat.

1895 The Japanese army crushes the Chinese at Wei-hai-Wei. Formosa and Port Arthur are ceded to Japan, but returned to China upon payment of a vast indemnity, part of which may have taken the form of Chinese agreement to assassinate the queen of Korea.

There is anarchy in the Turkish army: Armenians are massacred. Sultan Abdul Hamid II promises army reforms.

The Battle of Amba Alagi, Abyssinia: the Italian force is routed by a local tribal army.

War in Cuba: revolutionary forces fight the Spanish army, seeking independence.

1896 Italy's crumbling 'Protectorate Forces' are defeated again by Abyssinians at Adowa, forcing the Italian presence out of the country.

Turkish troops murder more Armenians, even on the streets of Constantinople.

The British army returns to Sudan, under command of General Kitchener.

An armed and armoured car, designed by E J Pennington, undergoes successful trials.

1897 Crete proclaims union with Greece. Turkey declares war on Greece but is defeated in Thessaly. Another 'Peace of Constantinople' secures armistice.

China is invaded again: Russians seize Port Arthur. The German naval bombardment of Kiao-Chou on the northern coast, is followed by occupation.

1898 Spanish–American war, fought largely in the Philippines.

China is persuaded to sign leases on Kowloon (by Britain) and Port Arthur (by Russia). Powerless, like Spain, against the huge naval guns in their harbours, some Chinese patriots form 'the Boxers', an anti-foreign/anti-western/anti-corruption resistance movement.

Horatio Herbert Kitchener's Western weaponry defeats Sudanese tribesmen on the Atbara river and at Omdurman, where a subaltern Winston Churchill participates, as he says, in 'the last full-scale cavalry charge made by the British army'.

1899

In the first Boer War, General Piet Joubert defeats a much larger British force at the Battle of Nicholson's Nek, and takes control of Ladysmith, in Natal. In one period of seven days, known as 'the Black Week' in the London press, Joubert thrice thrashes, with his horsemen, superior British forces at Stormberg, Magersfontein and Colenso. Canadian and Australian volunteer troops are called in to stop the galloping Boer riflemen.

1900 A weapon of the new century rises: Ferdinand von Zeppelin builds the first rigid dirigible, the zeppelin.

In China, the Boxers rise too, confronting the Europeans in a dozen Chinese cities. They even hold their own capital city Beijing for 55 days – during which they restrict foreign diplomats, soldiers, opium traders and Christian missionaries to the legation quarter of the city. The force that ends the Boxer rebellion brings 20,000 soldiers from eight nations to fight together. Admiral Edward Seymour, of Britain, and German General Alfred Graf von Waldersee command it. Soldiers, sailors and marines from Japan, Austria, Russia, Italy, France and the USA join the Royal Navy and the Junkers army in massacring approximately 50,000 Boxers and perhaps 25,000 Chinese imperial troops.

Lord Roberts of Kandahar is appointed to command in South Africa, with Kitchener of Khartoum as his chief of staff. Relief of Ladysmith, in February; Bloemfontein (the Boer 'capital') is captured in March; long-besieged Mafeking is relieved in May. The Boers are exhausted: their families become hostages – rounded up and concentrated in barbed-wire enclosures. The term 'concentration camp' enters humanity's nightmares. Britain annexes the Boer heartlands of Transvaal and the Orange Free State – Kitchener puts the stake through their urban hearts in Pretoria and Johannesburg. The Boers abandon formal military opposition, load their horses with ammunition and disappear into the veldt.

1901 The Boers begin systematic guerrilla warfare. Kitchener's conventional army has no answer to being hit-and-runned. Roberts sends Kitchener to propose armistice and amnesty to Boer leader Botha, at Middleburg.

1902 The Treaty of Vereeniging ends the Boer War. The Panama Canal under the construction: the USA to have 'perpetual control'.

1903 At Kittyhawk, in North Carolina, Orville and Wilbur Wright effectively demonstrate powered flight. So begins the age of aviation.

1904

Russo-Japanese War. Japan occupies Seoul and besieges Port Arthur. The Russian fleet attempts to break the blockade and is largely destroyed. The Russian army, also attempting to intervene, is badly beaten at Liaoyang, China.

1904 Radar is patented by Christian Hulsmeyer.

1905 Wireless communications are used in warfare for the first time by the Japanese army, followed shortly by Russian radio.

A general strike in Russia. The first workers' soviet (council) is formed in St Petersburg. Sailors mutiny on the battleship *Potemkin*.

1905

Port Arthur surrenders to the Japanese. Anti-czar demonstrations in St Petersburg are brutally crushed on 'Bloody Sunday' by czarist police and Cossack cavalry. The Russian army collapses at Mukden. The Russian navy is scattered in the Tsushima Straits. Russia sues for peace via a mediator – US President Theodor Roosevelt. Described by Toynbee as 'the first action for peace in American foreign policy since 1776'. The Treaty of Portsmouth (pictured) ends war and enshrines Japanese gains.

1906 US forces occupy Cuba.

1908 Civil war in Morocco: Abdul Hafid defeats his rival, Abdul Aziz, at the Battle of Marrakesh. Abdul Hafid becomes sultan.

In Turkey, radical army officers, 'the Young Turks', stage an uprising at Resina, Macedonia, and force elections for the Ottoman parliament – the Young Turks win with a large majority.

> ***"We will glorify war – the world's only hygiene – militarism, patriotism, the destructive acts of the anarchists, beautiful ideas worth dying for, and contempt for women"***

Manifesto of the Italian Futurists, *Le Figaro*, 20 February 1909.

1911 German sabres rattle. The kaiser tells an audience of Hamburgers that the older colonial powers will have to move over to make room for Germany's 'Place in the Sun'. He sends a gunboat, the *Panther*, to Agadir, Morocco, to meddle in the sultanate coup: an international crisis cartwheels into action as German motives are questioned.

War breaks out between Turkey and Italy. The Italian fleet bombards Tripoli's coast. An aircraft is used to drop sticks of dynamite – the first military use of the Wright brothers' flying machine. The Italian army decisively defeats Turkish forces in Tripoli and Cyrenaica, both annexed to a putative new Roman Empire.

1912 Revolution in central China. The Manchu dynasty, in power since 1644, falls. Pigtails (a symbol of serfdom) are abolished, a republic is proclaimed, ending the power and privilege of the Ch'ing. Military reorganization is immediately commenced, under General Chiang Kai-shek.

The Balkans become unstable, and Montenegro declares war on Turkey. Bulgaria and Serbia mobilize their armies.

1913 The Balkan War. The Bulgarian army seizes Adrianople, advancing across the Turkish border. The Turks seek armistice, signed in London, which is almost immediately broken. The Second Balkan War: Bulgaria attacks Serbia and Greece, and Russia declares war on Bulgaria. The Turks retake Adrianople and negotiate for a new border in Thrace. Serbia invades Albania.

1914 Archduke Franz Ferdinand, heir to the Austrian throne, and his wife are assassinated in Sarajevo. The Habsburg Empire is at war with Serbia. Germany declares war on Russia and France – the two-front war envisaged in the Von Schlieffen Plan of 1893 – and invades Belgium – they then turn to the east and crush Russia. Britain declares war on Germany.

1914
The German army's right-hook lays out Liège, then Lille, after battles at Manur and Mons. In the east, the Prussian 'holding' army rolls forward too, and smashes the Russians at Tannenberg and then near the Masurian Lakes. Only at the Marne river, in a bloody six-day battle, 9–15 September, is the German advance slowed. They reach west to the port of Antwerp and eastwards to Lodz, in Poland. Then, at Ypres, Von Hindenburg's troops are checked. Known to a generation of British squaddies as 'Wipers' and now as Ieper, Ypres (pictured) will become a scene of bitter trench warfare for the next four years.

> “ *Dear Friend,*
> *Again I say a terrible storm cloud hangs over Russia. Disaster, grief, murky darkness and no light. A whole ocean of tears, there is no counting them, and so much blood... We all drown in blood. The disaster is great, the misery infinite* ”

Grigory Rasputin to Nicholas II, July 1914.

1915 As the trenches extend, an armoured vehicle with caterpillar tracks is mooted to break the deadlock; it is code-named ‘Watertank’. Other inventions are used immediately: submarines begin to have a heavy impact on sea warfare. The British begin using the depth charge as an anti-submarine weapon. Paul Langevin develops sonar. The Fokker warplane becomes the first to have its machine guns synchronized with its propeller. Trench mortars are first used. Injuries from shrapnel propel a tetanus epidemic in the trenches. Anti-aircraft guns are introduced after German airships bomb East Anglian ports and zeppelins attack London. Flamethrowers are developed.

A second attritional battle is fought at Ypres. The Anzac assault at Gallipoli: Australian and New Zealand infantry are sent in to the bloodiest landing grounds as Winston Churchill’s plan to grab control of the Dardanelles collapses. Italy enters the war: it declares war on Austria, Hungary and Turkey – curiously, it does not care to engage against the Germans. A U-boat sinks the *Lusitania* passenger liner, drowning 100 American citizens: the Kriegsmarine will live to regret these torpedoes. Edith Cavell, a nurse, is executed by German firing squad in Brussels: another wrong decision. Czar Nicholas II takes personal command of the Russian army as the Germans drive into Warsaw and Brest-Litovsk: another seriously ill-informed policy decision. France and Britain change their high commands: Joseph Joffre and Douglas Haig respectively are appointed commander-in-chief. The British merchant navy loses over one million tons of shipping.

1916 Phosgene gas is developed. Mark I tanks are first used in action, completely ineffectually: their armour is penetrated by standard German machine guns, and they cannot bridge the average width of trenches in forward motion. The engines are rubbish too – unlike British armoured cars, which are Rolls-Royce Silver Ghosts with 9 mm plate steel all over.

Zeppelins drop bombs on Paris. The Easter Rising by Sinn Fein takes place in Dublin: the British army, already stretched, resorts to brutality as a containment measure. The Royal Navy finally brings the German High Seas Fleet to battle, at Jutland: both fleets claim victory. Off Orkney, Kitchener drowns when a mine sinks HMS *Hampshire*. Italy finally declares war on Germany. The British government changes: David Lloyd George, a warrior of the Cymraeg, becomes prime minister – he rejects a German truce note and US President Woodrow Wilson's appeal for peace.

British merchant shipping loses over 1,600,000 tons in 1916.

Elsewhere, Francisco 'Pancho' Villa, a Mexican revolutionary general, 'invades' the USA with 300 guerrillas and raids Columbus, New Mexico. Brigadier-General John Pershing pursues him with 6,000 troops, but cannot find him. Pershing is promoted to full general, and, in due course, command of the US army in Europe.

THE RUSSIAN REVOLUTION
1917

The Russian revolution of 1917 actually took place in two parts. The Bolshevik revolution happened in February, when the Czar, Nicholas II, abdicated, and members of the Duma (the legislative assembly) took control over Russia in order to form a provisional government. The second happened later that year, when the Bolsheviks – a former faction of the Marxist Russian Social Democrat Labour Party, led by Vladimir Lenin – seized control and overthrew the provisional government. Both phases were part of a revolution aimed at replacing a regime that had exploited and oppressed the working population for centuries. The revolution had the effect of totally transforming the nature of Russian society, and the Russian state. It replaced the Czarist autocracy and led ultimately to the establishment of the Soviet Union. Following the Bolshevik uprising, a civil war erupted between Red (communist) (pictured) and White (nationalist) factions. Ultimately, the Bolsheviks were victorious, paving the way for the establishment of the USSR.

1917 February 'Revolution' in Russia: the czar abdicates on 16 March, a victim of his own cultivated ignorance. The USA finally goes to war with Germany, Wilson's declaration is jointly signed by Cuba. Portugal and China have also now joined the 'Allies'.

The Battle of Passchendaele, also known as the third battle of Ypres: British, ANZAC (Australia and New Zealand), Canadian and South African units engage with the German army. The Luftwaffe – German air force – attacks London with biplane bombers. The Italian army are routed at Caporetto.

The October Revolution in Russia: the absent czar's puppet premier, Kerensky, is ousted. Lenin is appointed chief commissar,

Trotsky is foreign minister: he negotiates the Treaty of Brest-Litovsk – a truce on the eastern front. US troops arrive in Europe: Wilson belatedly remembers to declare war on Austria-Hungary. The first serious tank battle at Cambrai.

British merchant shipping loses over four million tons during 1917.

1918

Improvized aircraft carriers are developed at the end of the First World War for scouting reconnaissance and air defence. The Luftwaffe assembles 1,388 strike aircraft to form an attack on Britain – just 15 years after Kittyhawk. The RAF is separated and reorganized to replace the Royal Flying Corps (formerly part of the British army, just as the Second World War US Army Air Force evolved into the USAF). The Germans launch their largest-ever offensive on the western front, and a thousand-plane bombing raid on Paris. The second Battle of the Marne leads to Allied breakthrough. Germany and Austria agree to Wilson's demand that they should retreat to their own territory before an armistice is signed. The German fleet mutinies at Kiel – creating a fear of a 'Red Revolution'. The Germans suspend submarine warfare. An armistice is signed on 11 November.

1918 Counter-revolutionary war in Russia; Red Guards versus White Guards. The Soviet government executes Former Czar Nicholas, and the entire Romanoff family.

At least twenty million people died as a direct result of warfare between August 1914 and November 1918.

“They shall not grow old, as we that are left grow old: Age shall not weary them, nor the years condemn. At the going down of the sun and in the morning We will remember them”

Laurence Binyon 'For the Fallen', 1914

1919 A peace conference at Versailles. President Wilson presides over the first meeting of 'The League of Nations', in Paris.

The Soviet 'Red army' drives White Guards into the Crimean peninsula, taking Ufa – White resistance crumbles. The Soviet army turns to Finland, and invades.

British armies are free to restart conflict with native forces in India and Afghanistan, and to support White Russians in Murmansk. The Kriegsmarine fleet is scuttled in the harbour of Scapa Flow: German delegates then sign the Versailles peace treaty.

Withdrawals by British forces from Murmansk and Americans from Archangel, as White Russian resistance to the Soviet Revolution proves pointless.

1920 Red Army mopping-up operations: the last White stronghold at Odessa is taken. The League of Nations is duly constituted: the US Senate immediately votes against joining. League headquarters are moved from Paris to Geneva.

1921 Guilio Douhet, Italian general and theorist on the strategy of aerial warfare, publishes *The Command of the Air.*

1921
Retired American army officer John T Thompson (pictured here in 1922) patents his rotary sub-machine gun – the Tommy gun.

1922 J F Fuller publishes *Lectures on Field Service Regulations III*, under which unprepossessing title he lays the foundations for armoured warfare. In the First World War he served as chief of staff to the Royal Tank Corps, and between the wars he convinced many that tanks would be the wave of the future, including Liddell Hart, Georgi Zhukov and Erwin Rommel.

1926 The first liquid-propellant rocket is launched.

1927 Italy accomplishes the first instance of planned military parachuting after adapting escape parachutes for the task.

B Kellogg, US secretary of state, advocates a binding pact on sovereign governments for the renunciation of war between nations.

> **“ *Friends, raise your right arm and cry out with me proudly, eager for the struggle, and loyal unto death, ‘Heil Hitler’* ”**

Gregor Strasser, 9 January 1927.

1928 Kellogg-Briand Pact, outlawing war, is signed in Paris by 65 countries.

1929 Basil Liddell Hart publishes *The Decisive Wars of History*, which will later develop into his celebrated treatise on 'strategy', probably the most influential 20th-century book on conventional warfare.

1930 Britain, France, Italy and the USA sign the treaty on naval disarmament.

1931 Deuterium is discovered.

1932 Approximately 17,000 ex-servicemen occupy Washington DC to demand the cashing of their Veterans' Bonus Certificates – their demobilisation money. The 'Doughboys' of the First World War – mainly infantry – are refused their entitlements and driven from the city by the largest US army cavalry action since the 19th century.

Similar street scenes occur in Germany, when Hitler refuses Hindenburg's offer to become vice-chancellor after the Nazi Party gains the majority of seats in the Reichstag elections.

1933
The first practical helicopter is developed by Igor Sikorsky (pictured). The launch of the first purpose-built aircraft carrier, USS *Ranger*.

1934 Robert Watson-Watt develops a practical radar for aircraft detection.

“I was a little shocked at the faces, especially those of the women, when Hitler finally appeared on the balcony for a moment. They reminded me of the crazed expressions I saw once in the back country of Louisiana on the faces of some Holy Rollers who were about to hit the trail. They looked up at him as if he were a messiah, their faces transformed into something positively inhuman”

William Shirer, an American journalist at the Nuremberg Nazi Party Rally, 1934, from *Berlin Diary*, 1941.

1935 The Nazis repudiate the Versailles Treaty and reintroduce compulsory military service.

Wehrmacht (united German forces) develops the first armoured (Panzer) divisions. Revenge for Amba Alagi, 1895: Italy invades Abyssinia. Council of the League of Nations reprimands Mussolini as an 'aggressor'.

The Luftwaffe is totally reorganized by First World War fighter-pilot Hermann Goering.

1936 Erich Ludendorff, head of the German army during the First World War, publishes *The Nation at War*, one of Hitler's favourite books. It sets out a vision of future total war in which the nation is servant to its armed forces.

Wehrmacht occupies Rhineland. Italy wins the Abyssinian War, and annexes the entire country.

1936
The Spanish Civil War begins in July. Fascist General Francisco Franco takes Badajzoz: Madrid is besieged.

1937 Poland refuses Hitler's demand for the return of Danzig (Gdansk). Franco's forces take Malaga and Gijon. They are assisted by Condor Legion – German 'volunteers', commanded by Wolfram von Richtofen, son of the first world war fighter ace, aka the Red Baron, who led the 'Flying Circus'. The Luftwaffe – at the behest of Franco's Nationalists – carried out a bombing raid against the Basque town of Guernica in northern Spain, killing more than 1,600 civilians. Spain's Republican government commissioned Picasso, the country's most famous artist, to create a mural commemorating the atrocity. First shown in the Spanish Pavilion at the Paris International Exposition, in July 1937, Picasso's *Guernica* became the 20th century's most famous anti-war image. It now hangs at the Reina Sofia gallery in Madrid.

Japan invades China, seizing Beijing, Tientsin, Shanghai, Nanking and Hangchow. The League of Nations instructs Japan to withdraw its troops from China.

1937
Picasso, a Republican, was trapped in Paris during the coming German occupation of France. His artistic fame protected him from most political persecution, but there is a fine story of a Gestapo man on a regular harassment visit to Picasso's Paris studio in 1941, who found a postcard of *Guernica* and demanded of this 'degeneracy': Did you do this? To which Pablo replied, Oh no: you did. Take one as a souvenir.

1938 The Japanese army reaches Tsingtao, and installs a Chinese puppet government. Japan walks out of the League of Nations and takes over the major port of Canton.

British Prime Minister Neville Chamberlain flies to Berchtesgarden to hear Hitler's 'final territorial demand in Europe'. He agrees that Sudeten German speakers in Czechoslovakia should join the Third Reich. Wehrmacht occupies Sudetenland. Hungary, a German ally, annexes southern Slovakia. Keitel, Guderian and Halder are appointed to high command of the Wehrmacht. They represent the dive-bomber, panzer tank and half-track – the precision artillery, mobile armour and fast-moving infantry that will transform land warfare into *blitzkrieg* (lightning war).

1939 Hitler proves to have some more final demands. The Wehrmacht marches into Bohemia and Moraina, places northern Slovakia under 'protection' and annexes Memel. Renunciation of a non-aggression pact with Poland and a naval agreement with Britain is replaced by a non-aggression pact with the USSR and 10-year alliance with Italy.

The Japanese occupy Hainan and blockade the British concession at Tientsin.

Italy invades Albania.

The Spanish Civil War ends, Franco is victorious. Spain leaves the League of Nations, as does Hungary.

Britain and Poland sign the 'Treaty of Mutual Assistance'.

1939

Germany invades Poland on 1 September; Britain and France declare war on Germany on 3 September. Wehrmacht overruns Poland's archaic army, takes Warsaw and reaches Brest-Litovsk. Using the same maps as 1914, Soviet forces invade Poland from the east and then Finland to the north. The Battle of the River Plate: German pocket battleship *Graf Spee* is forced to scuttle in Uruguayan waters by three light cruisers of the British and New Zealand navies.

1940 Finland negotiates a peace treaty with Soviet leader Stalin in return for ceding Karelia. Wehrmacht takes Denmark and Norway, invades Holland, Belgium and Luxembourg, then France.

Winston Churchill becomes British prime minister, he offers 'nothing but blood, toil, tears and sweat'.

The Low Countries capitulate. Evacuation from Dunkirk of 340,000 British and Allied troops, 29 May to 3 June. The Germans enter Paris on 14 June. The new French government, under Pétain, offers armistice and all of northern France to Hitler. Italy declares war on France and Britain. The Royal Navy sinks the French fleet, which has fled to Oran. Churchill signs an agreement with de Gaulle (Free French) and Polish government-in-exile, led by Sikorski, to continue resistance.

The Battle of Britain: the Luftwaffe is narrowly defeated by Spitfires and Hurricanes of RAF Fighter Command, as the Germans strive for air ascendancy over the English Channel to enable 'Operation Sea Lion' – the German invasion of Britain. Hitler replicates Napoleon's decisions of 1804: he cancels 'Sea Lion' and orders preparation for Operation Barbarossa – the invasion of Russia.

London Blitz – heavy bombing raids on many other British cities also. U-boat warfare in the North Atlantic sinks a million tons of

Allied merchant shipping. The British 8th army, under Wavell, faces the Afrika Corps led by Rommel in North Africa.

Plutonium is discovered.

1941 General Wavell occupies Benghazi. British forces face the Italians in Abyssinia. American negotiators gouge vast concessions from Churchill in return for 'Lend-Lease' of 50 decrepit First World War destroyers. Despite astounding efforts by the Canadian navy, U-boats are ascendant in the Battle of the Atlantic.

Rommel counterattacks in Libya, retakes Benghazi and besieges Tobruk. German paratroopers lead a remarkable invasion of Crete, and the Royal Navy is chased away by Stuka dive-bombers – HMS *Kelly* is sunk, as is the Royal Navy's most famous ship, HMS *Hood*, when she confronts the German battleship *Bismarck* in the Denmark Strait.

Churchill's famous three-word order for total concentration of all available resources to one end: 'Sink the *Bismarck*!' HMS *Rodney* does just so.

Barbarossa launches the biggest single military campaign ever known. Wehrmacht captures Minsk, Smolensk and Tallinn – Panzers race across the Ukraine, taking Kiev, Orel, Odessa and Kharkov. They then advance to the outskirts of Leningrad and continue towards Moscow.

1941

7 December: Japanese bomb Pearl Harbor. They sink the USS *Arizona* and inflict heavy casualties. Japanese torpedo bombers also cripple the Royal Navy: battleships *Prince of Wales* and *Repulse* are sunk off Singapore. Hong Kong surrenders.

1942 Under the banner of 'the United Nations' a total of 26 Allied nations pledge not to make separate peace treaties with either Germany or Japan. The Japanese capture Singapore, Java and Rangoon, they invade the Philippines and occupy Bataan. Thousands of American and Filipino prisoners die in the 'Bataan Death March' – the first of many Japanese atrocities against prisoners of war. Equally disreputable actions are perpetrated in the US against Nisei, Japanese-American citizens: over 100,000 are driven from the Pacific coastal regions to concentration camps far inland. The first major sea conflict between aircraft carriers, the Battle of the Coral Sea, is followed by another American victory at Midway. US marines make a bloody landing on Guadalcanal. Rommel takes Tobruk after dogged resistance from Australian 'diggers'. Montgomery takes command of the 8th army, grinds down Rommel's tank army at El Alamein and forces a full retreat. The Germans lose Tobruk and Benghazi.

They also lose any possibility of resolving the war without total surrender by instituting the 'Final Solution' – the murder of millions of Jews in gas chambers. This war becomes ever more obscene. Stalemate at Stalingrad: Wehrmacht and the Red army are locked in a desperate street-by-street deadlock, which neither can break.

The Soviets introduce rocket artillery. The Germans develop the assault rifle, but they were not widely adopted until after the Second World War because they lacked the power of standard rifles.

US Manhattan Project begins in order to develop the first atomic bomb. The anti-tank rocket, or bazooka, is invented. Before the bazooka, only anti-tank grenades or 'elephant guns' would damage well-armoured tanks – but even these performed poorly. Aircraft carriers become the major offensive arm of naval power. American carrier-borne airpower will tip the balance in the Pacific.

"A fairly barbaric practice will be used...one that cannot be precisely described. Not many of the Jews will be left over. Roughly speaking, one can be sure that 60 per cent of them will have to be liquidated, while we will be able to put only 10 per cent into labour detachments"

Joseph Goebbels, diary entry 27 March 1942

1943 The United States Marine Corps (USMC) drives the Japanese from Guadalcanal. A total of 22 Japanese ships are sunk during a single night in the Battle of the Bismarck Sea.

The Red army destroys Wehrmacht, south-east of Stalingrad. General Paulus surrenders, against Hitler's orders; he orders a scorched-earth policy during any German retreat. The biggest tank battles ever occur around Kursk.

Eisenhower takes command of Allied armies in North Africa – the British advance from Tripoli links up with Americans from Tunis and Bizerte in the west.

The 'Dam Busters' raid: RAF Lancasters use amazing 'bouncing bombs' to attack Ruhr dam. The amphibious assault from North Africa, through Sicily, on what Churchill calls 'the soft underbelly of the crocodile'. Palermo is seized, then Messina. From there, the assault reaches the Italian mainland in Salerno Bay. The Italian government are weak at the knees as the US 5th army captures Naples. German forces move south down the Italian peninsula. Mussolini is deposed. Marshall Badoglio heads a new government, surrenders to Eisenhower and decides to declare war on Germany.

The Red Army crosses Dnieper, north of Kiev, and seizes Smolensk. Wehrmacht discipline and supply lines smashed by Russian winter.

Germany is bombed round the clock – by the RAF all night and by USAAF Flying Fortresses in daylight.

1944 The first use of air-launched, radio command guided anti-ship missiles. The first V-1 flying bomb used by Germany against the UK. V-2 rockets are used by Germany: 1,050 fall on Britain. The first German military jet, the Messerschmidt, is used in battle. Acoustic homing torpedoes are developed.

In Italy, there are Allied landings at Nettuno and Anzio. Monte Cassino monastery is fortified by the Germans: it has to be obliterated by USAAF bombers before being taken on 4 June. Rome, Open City, is liberated. The 8th army reaches Florence.

In Germany, there are 'thousand-bomber raids' on Berlin, dropping nearly 3,000 tons of explosive and incendiaries per raid.

The eastern front – Red Army offensives in Ukraine and Crimea. Sebastopol is liberated, then Minsk, where over 100,000 Germans are taken prisoner.

The Pacific – Americans complete the conquest of the Solomon and Marshall Islands and land on Guam. There is heavy fighting in Burma. MacArthur lands in the Philippines – twice, so that film cameras can record his 'return'.

D-day, 6 June – 700 ships and 4,000 landing craft cross Manche in Operation Overlord, the invasion of Normandy. There is bitter fighting around Caen. De Gaulle returns to Paris on 25 August. Operation Market Garden – the biggest ever airborne assault, designed to seize Rhine bridges. The Battle of the Bulge, in Ardennes – the last major German counter-attack, blunted by stubborn resistance by troops of US 101st Division at Bastogne. The American 3rd army, under G S Patton, breaks Panzerarmees from Cherbourg to the Rhine.

Russians link with Tito's Yugoslav partisans and take Belgrade. They enter Hungary and besiege Budapest. They arrive too late in Warsaw to help the Jewish Rising in the Ghetto. France regains Lorraine. Ho Chi Minh declares Vietnam independent of France.

1945 Russians in Silesia, take Krakow, Tilsit and reach the Oder river. The British 2nd army crosses the Rhine. The Americans take Manila and land on Okinawa. Franklin D Roosevelt dies, Harry S. Truman succeeds him as president. US and USSR troops meet at Torgau. The United Nations Charter is signed in San Francisco. The League of Nations holds its final meeting in Geneva and turns over its assets to the UN. Mussolini is shot, and then hung, by Italian partisans. Hitler commits suicide on 30 April. The German army, in the south (Italian front), surrenders on May Day, Berlin capitulates on 2 May, formal surrender of OKW (Oberkommandwehrmacht) on 7 May. 'VE Day' – 8th May – Victory in Europe.

The British Labour Party wins a landslide election majority. Clement Attlee replaces Churchill at the Potsdam Conference with Truman and Stalin. Germany is divided into four control areas, Berlin into three. Fascist Spain is excluded from the UN.

The US drops atomic bombs on Hiroshima, 6 August, and Nagasaki, 9 August. Japanese Emperor Hirohito has already signed an instrument to cease hostilities. Japan surrenders on 14 August – 'VJ Day'.

THE ATOMIC BOMB
1945

The atomic bomb has only been used twice in the history of warfare, both times by the United States at the order of President Harry S Truman, against the Empire of Japan, during the last days of the Second World War, in August 1945.

By the beginning of August 1945, the US had been persistently firebombing Japan for six months, wiping out 67 cities and killing approximately 500,000 people. When the time came to step-up their offensive, Truman found there was little else they could do besides unleashing the most destructive weapon on the planet – the atomic bomb.

The bombs had killed a total of 140,000 people in Hiroshima, and a further 80,000 in Nagasaki by the end of 1945. At least half of these people died during the initial blast, but since then thousands more have died from injuries sustained in the bombing, or from diseases as a result of exposure to radiation. An overwhelming majority of the victims were civilians.

End of the Second World War. The number of war dead is estimated at 38 million – 25 million of them Russian, plus approximately 10 million dead in Nazi concentration camps.

To what purpose is this waste?

Matthew 26, v.8

George Smith Patton, an unpopular man but the greatest field commander and fighting general of the war, dies after being involved in a road accident before Christmas. He chose to be buried among the men of his 3rd army who were killed at the Battle of the Bulge in Hamm Cemetery, Luxembourg.

One of the four original signatories to the Charter of the new UN was Jan Smuts, prime minister of South Africa. In his biography, W K Hancock addressed the victory:

"When the war ended, Smuts welcomed the atomic bomb: At least a discovery has been made which should put war out of court for good and all … So I am not without hope of the future even if that hope is based, so to say, on despair – human nature being at last coerced into proper behaviour, where no other appeal would do."

Post 1945, the use of radar and techniques to quickly find artillery firing positions led to rapid advances in self-propelled artillery.

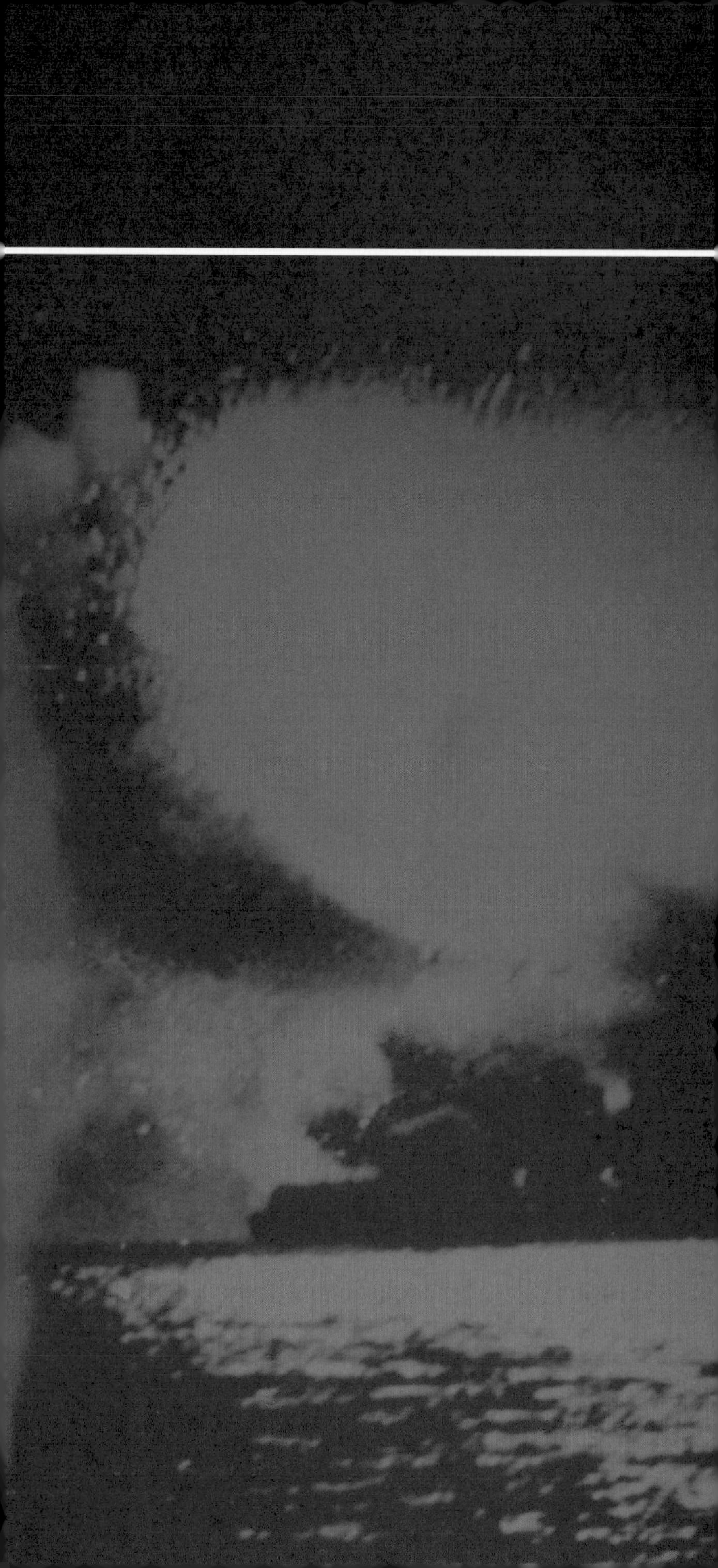

VJ DAY – PRESENT DAY

1946–Present day

1946 Churchill gives his 'Iron Curtain' speech in Fulton, Missouri. The Nuremburg War Crimes Tribunal sentences Halder, von Ribbentrop and Goering to death. Goering commits suicide by poison the night before he is due to be executed.

1948 War in Palestine as the state of Israel is proclaimed.

1949 The Soviet Union develops its own atomic device.

1950 War in Korea. An army from the north invades South Korea and captures Seoul. The UN appoints General Douglas MacArthur to command an 'expulsion force'. Nearly all-American, the force links with South Korean troops and retakes Seoul. Chinese forces join the war.

1951 North Korean forces break through the 38th parallel, they retake Seoul and reject American peace offers. MacArthur is relieved of command. UN forces rally to recapture 'Heartbreak Ridge', north of Yanguu. Armistice talks at Panmunjom fail.

1952 There are anti-British riots in Egypt as Churchill announces that Britain also has the atomic bomb. Jomo Kenyatta and Mau-Mau start anti-colonial war in Kenya.

1953

In the Korean War, the jet aircraft makes its first wartime flights from aircraft carriers, and helicopters are first used on a large scale. The first US hydrogen bomb is successfully tested. Long-range intercontinental ballistic missiles are developed by the USA. The first nuclear submarine, the Nautilus, is laid down.

The Korean War ends in stalemate after successful UN/US landings at Inchon. A peace treaty is signed at Panmunjom. USA/South Korea sign a 'mutual defence treaty'.

1954 Colonel Nasser seizes power in Egypt: more riots against foreign control of Suez Canal.

The French colonial army is locked in struggle with Viet-minh communists/freedom fighters. The French garrison are cut off and defeated at Die n Bien Phu. Ho Chi Minh's army occupies Hanoi.

The US and Canada agree to build radar stations across far northern DEW line (Distant Early Warning) to provide warning of approaching (Soviet) aircraft or missiles over the Arctic. The USSR tests a hydrogen bomb.

> ***"Local defenses must be reinforced by the further deterrent of massive retaliatory power...the basic decision was to defend primarily upon a great capacity to retaliate, instantly, by means and at places of our choosing"***

US Secretary of State John Foster Dulles, speaking about the development of nuclear weapons, 12 Jan 1954

1955 The US Air Force Academy is established, modelled on West Point (army) and Anapolis (navy).

1956 Israel is still struggling against Arab forces, despite a UN-arranged truce with Jordan and ceasefires with Lebanon and Syria. Israeli troops move into Egypt and invade the Sinai Peninsula. Nasser seizes control of the Suez Canal. There is a secret joint reaction from Britain, France and Israel. Despite Anglo-French air strikes against Egyptian airfields, there is fighting along the canal line for a week before pressure from both USSR and USA effects a ceasefire.

1957 Israeli forces withdraw from Sinai and hand over the Gaza strip to UN control. UN Secretary-General Dag Hammarskjöld influences Nasser to allow UN teams to clear the Canal – some sense of international law in the ascendant. Britain explodes a thermonuclear bomb in the central Pacific.

1958 Fidel Castro and Ché Guevara declare 'total war' against the Batista government in Cuba.

The Soviet Union explodes what is still (in 2008) the most powerful thermonuclear bang on earth.

1959 Castro's forces take Havana, and Batista runs away to the Dominican Republic. Castro nationalizes American-owned sugar mills.

A Soviet rocket reaches the Moon. Lunik III photographs lunar surface in detail.

1960 USS *Triton*, a nuclear submarine, completes the first circumnavigation of the world underwater.

1961 Multi-role fighter/attack aircraft begin to replace fighter/fighter-bomber aircraft. The *Long Beach*, the first nuclear-powered surface warship, is commissioned.

In Cuba, exiled opponents of the Castro revolution land at the Bay of Pigs, and are bloodily repulsed. The entire fiasco – planning, training and supply – is funded by the CIA.

1962 The USSR agrees to send arms to Cuba in exchange for harbours for its fishing fleet. This is extended to the installation of missile bases, which US President Kennedy demands be dismantled. The US navy establishes blockades and 'quarantines' Cuba. There is a real possibility of nuclear war for 13 days in October. Then Soviet premier, Khrushchev, backs down, agrees to remove missiles, Soviet aircraft – and even the fishing boats.

1963 President Kennedy sends 3,000 troops to impose martial law in an urgent race to stop murders and beatings of American citizens in Birmingham, Alabama. (The dead and wounded are all black citizens.) He is assassinated on 22 November. By the end of 1963, North American early warning radar system is set up at DEW line, to detect incoming Soviet missiles.

1964 Civil war in Cyprus, the Turkish air force strikes at Nicosia. General Grivas becomes the commander of Greek Cypriot forces.

The US destroyer *Maddox* is allegedly attacked by North Vietnamese patrol boats on 2 August, in the Gulf of Tonkin. American aircraft bomb North Vietnam in reprisal. On 7 August, US Congress passes the 'Gulf of Tonkin' resolution, giving President Johnson almost unlimited war powers in south-east Asia. China explodes its first atomic bomb on 7 October and Nikita Khrushchev is deposed on 14 October. When he defeats Goldwater, two weeks later, by the widest margin in electoral history, Lyndon B Johnson, a Texan, takes over as president of the United States of America.

1965
Operation 'Rolling Thunder' commences, with sustained and heavy bombing of Vietnam. A total of 62 combat battalions comprising over 200,000 troops are sent to South Vietnam, under command of General William Westmoreland (pictured, centre). The Americans are victorious in the first big conventional clash or 'pitched battle', of the war, that US firepower can dominate – at the Battle of La Trang Valley.

1966 'Rolling Thunder' continues with attacks by carrier-borne aircraft, and B-52s are extended to oil depots near Hanoi and the port of Haiphong. American troop strength reaches 400,000. Guerrilla warfare by the Viet Cong pins down this vast army. Westmoreland complains that the Vietnamese 'won't stand and fight'.

Israeli and Jordanian forces clash – heavy fighting in the Hebron Valley area.

Harvard professor Thomas Schelling publishes *Arms and Influence*.

1967 The first use of surface-to-surface missiles in combat. Also, during the Vietnam War, surface-to-air missiles are effectively deployed for the first time, and hovercraft are used on inland waterways. American troop strength reaches half a million.

France launches its first nuclear submarine *La Redoutable*.

1967
The Six Day War – the Israeli Air Force achieves a phenomenal 48 to 1 kill-ratio, destroying most Arab air forces on the ground. Israeli infantry takes the old city of Jerusalem. Israeli armour seizes control of the Sinai Peninsula and then approaches the Suez Canal. Resolute attacks on the hugely superior Syrian numbers gain IDF (Israel Defence Force) unexpected control over the Golan Heights, eliminating, for the first time since Israel was founded in 1948, the dominance of Syrian artillery over the northern half of the country.

1968 The French army, back in action, is used to support CRS (Cossack Repressive Section of Gendarmerie) in horrific violence against student demonstrators. Most of France is appalled. *Les évenements* is supported by general strike. Huge demonstrations around the world against serial Western interventions in south-east Asia.

The North Korean navy is back in action: USS *Pueblo*, an American spyship, is arrested in North Korean territorial waters. Her crew are released when the USA apologizes for the violation.

In Britain, Prime Minister Harold Wilson meets controversial Rhodesian leader, Ian Smith aboard HMS *Fearless*. Zimbabwean liberation forces continue a vicious bush war: Rhodesian Salou Scouts exceed their brutality, as a bush fighter named Mugabe establishes a reputation for blood lust.

The Red Army is back in action: Soviet and Warsaw Pact tanks roll into Czechoslovakia after liberalizing Czech leader Dubček abolishes press censorship and resists other pressures from Moscow.

The North Vietnamese Liberation Army gives Westmoreland what he asked for: in the Tet offensive, NVLA regulars seize Hué and they support 'Charlie' (Victor-Charles, V-C, the Viet Cong) in attacks on a dozen South Vietnamese towns and cities. Hué is retaken after 26 days of the war's heaviest fighting. Westmoreland asks for an additional 206,000 troops.

Senator Robert Kennedy is assassinated.

MY LAI MASSACRE
1969

The My Lai massacre took place over three hours in the morning of 16 March 1968, in the South Vietnamese village of My Lai, when more than 500 unarmed civilians were brutally murdered by rampaging US troops. The massacre was part of Operation Phoenix, a search-and-destroy mission designed to root out communist fighters who were apparently hiding-out within fertile Viet Cong territory. Most of the victims of the My Lai massacre were women and children, some of whom were beaten, sexually abused or dismembered post mortem. To make matters worse, there had been no enemy fire. Not a single shot was fired at the men of the Charlie Company, a unit of the American Division's 11th infantry brigade, as they entered My Lai. The Viet Cong unit they were looking for failed to materialize. By this point in the war, the Americans were deeply entrenched in their battle against communism in South Vietnam. The Viet Cong guerrillas and the North Vietnamese army had launched a joint attack known as the Tet offensive, Washington maintained that America could win the war for democracy, but on the ground,morale was dangerously low. Charlie Company had been in Vietnam for three months, and in that time they had sustained 28 casualties, including 5 dead. Some of their number had already begun using brutal tactics – but they were allowed to get away with it. On entry to My Lai, the soldiers of the Charlie Company went berserk, gunning down unarmed men, women, children and even babies. Families huddled together for safety but were shown no mercy. Even those who surrendered were ruthlessly murdered. It is important to note that 120 American soldiers opted out of the massacre, and played no part in the violence, but the troop commander, Lieutenant William Calley, didn't hold back. He was eventually brought to trial for his part in the murders. When news of the slaughter reached the outside world it sent shockwaves through the American establishment and further de-stabilized public feeling about the war. The American pubic simply could not believe that their soldiers were capable of such brutality.

1969
Violent street fighting between Catholics and Protestants in Northern Ireland. The British Army commits troops to quell rioting.

1969 The new US president, Richard Nixon authorizes the secret bombing of Cambodia. Newspeak US Secretary of Defence Laird invents the term 'Vietnamization' to cover proposed troop withdrawals – 25,000 (4.7%) is the grand initial gesture. Ho Chi Minh dies in Hanoi on 3 September. He had been fighting French, Japanese and American 'imperialism' since his first trip to Paris in 1912. The My Lai massacre of Vietnamese civilians is revealed – it has been covered up for a year. Many ordinary Americans are outraged, and huge demonstrations take place in 24 cities, culminating in a massive march on Washington in November. Nixon dismisses them, praising the 'silent majority'. He also announces that another 25,000 troops will return by the end of the year.

Palestine Liberation Organization guerrillas continue to fight against Israeli occupation. New Chairman Yasser Arafat shifts his main force from the occupied West Bank into Jordan.

> ***"The conventional army loses if it does not win. The guerrilla wins if he does not lose"***

Henry Kissinger, Jan. 1969

1970 Civil war ends in Nigeria. Federalist army triumphs over secessionist Biafra.

Nixon proposes 'standstill ceasefire'. American combat deaths in October number 24, the lowest monthly toll since mid 1965. Lieutenant W Calley faces trial for the My Lai massacre. The US troop strength is down to 280,000 men by Christmas.

1971 US planes bomb Viet Cong supply routes – the 'Ho Chi Minh trail' in neutral Cambodia; fly strike missions in support of trepid ARVN (South Vietnam) forces fighting illegally in Laos. In the biggest ever bombing raids against North Vietnam, Hanoi is struck daily, Haiphong harbour mined. Another 100,000 American ground troops are withdrawn during the year.

The British Ulster army comes under fire after the introduction of two draconian policies: preventive detention and internment without trial.

1972 East Pakistan emerges as the sovereign state of Bangladesh.

The British Army is used as an instrument of direct rule in Northern Ireland. A total of 467 civilians are killed there during the year.

German soldiers are in action for the first time since 1945. Nine Jews are killed in Munich after the Palestine Liberation Organization takes hostages.

In Vietnam, the NVLA launches a brief offensive across the demilitarized zone. Nixon authorizes closure of ports in North Vietnam by indiscriminate use of air-laid mines. Hanoi is blitzed by N-52s between 15 April and 8 October. The US Secretary of State, Kissinger, announces that 'peace is at hand' on 1 November. Nixon is re-elected, by a landslide, on 7 November. Bombing resumes soon after.

1973
Vietnam ceasefire is signed on 23 January. The USA spent $109,500,000,000 on the war. Fighting continued after the ceasefire.

1973 Lyndon Baines Johnson dies.

In the Middle East, Arabs attack Israel again, and breakthrough at a dozen points. Israel Defence Force counter-attacks push back all fronts beyond their original positions. They are described as 'Stalingrad' fighting – the worst conditions of all the Arab–Israeli conflicts. Ceasefires break down several times.

Native Americans occupy the South Dakota hamlet of Wounded Knee for 70 days.

In Chile, President Salvador Allende Gossens is overthrown by military junta. He dies fighting for his office – literally, from behind his desk, with a sub-machine gun in his hands.

1974 Greek Cypriot nationalists overthrow the government of Archbishop Makarios, who flees the island. Turkish armed forces launch a huge amphibious and airborne invasion; seize control of all of northern Cyprus and advance to the capital, Nicosia.

Work begins on clearing the Suez Canal, which has been closed by block-ships since the Six Day War of 1967.

President Thieu of South Vietnam declares that the war has restarted.

1975 In Vietnam, the NVLA takes control of Phuoc Long province, north of Saigon and captures the provincial capital, Banmethuot on 11 March. Thieu orders the northern half of South Vietnam to be abandoned, then reverses the order – Hué to be held at all costs. NVLA takes the city in five days. The 'Frequent Wind', evacuation of the last Americans from Saigon. NVLA Colonel Bui Tin's armoured column takes the city on 30 April.

In Cambodian territorial waters, the US spy ship *Mayaguez* is boarded and escorted to harbour. B-52s bomb Phnompenh in reprisal. A total of 38 US marines die in the 'rescue' of 39 seamen, after agreement that they would be returned.

USAF withdraws its last combat aircraft from Taiwan (Formosa) and the army reduces its troops there to fewer than 3,000 men.

“ *Television brought the brutality of war into the comfort of the living room. Vietnam was lost in the living rooms of America – not on the battlefields of Vietnam* ”

Marshall McLuhan, *Montreal Gazette*, 16 May 1975

1976 The SALT Treaty II (Strategic Arms Limitation Talks) is signed by the USA and USSR. It limits the size of underground nuclear explosions and provides, for the first time, for on-site inspection of compliance.

Vietnam is reunited after 22 years of separation. Saigon is renamed Ho Chi Minh City.

South Africa's white army kills hundreds of black protesters against apartheid, from Soweto to Johannesburg to Cape Town and Crossroads.

Syrian troops and Lebanese Christians in bloody conflict against Palestinian guerrillas and Lebanese Muslims in southern Lebanon. The Syrian army takes control of Beirut, Tripoli, Sarda and all inter-city highways.

1977 Pakistani army general, Zia ul-Haq overthrows the government of Zulfiquar Ali Bhutto and imposes martial law.

1978 There are tensions between the Socialist Republic of Vietnam and the Khmer Rouge regime, led by the barbarous Pol Pot, in Cambodia. Ho Chi Minh's successors demand that the 'Killing Fields' stop, as does the UN. China demurs, but Vietnam forces invade Cambodia anyway. The NVLA is battle-hardened and brilliantly disciplined: the butchers of the Khmer Rouge are crushed. The NVLA discovers mass graves of over three million Khmer Rouge victims.

1979 Jimmy Carter describes the SALT-2 limitation treaty as 'a victory in the battle for peace'.

Bloody civil war in Nicaragua: President Somoza is overthrown by Sandinistas.

1980 Red Army in Afghanistan: Soviet *spetznatz* (special forces) are engaged in fierce clashes with Mujaheddin guerrillas in the Hindu Kush mountains. The UN calls on the Kremlin to withdraw its troops.

Iraq invades Iran, attempting to gain control of Abadan and the Shatt al Arab waterway: the war will last throughout the 1990s. Casualties will total over two million.

1980
American hostages are held in the Teheran embassy. The rescue mission fails to get anywhere near Teheran. By contrast, when terrorists seize the Iranian Embassy in London, taking 19 hostages, the SAS (Special Air Services) storm the building and rescue everybody.

1981 Iran releases all 52 American hostages.

Civil war rages in Lebanon. Syrian 'Arab Deterrent Force' fights Islamic guerrillas and Saad Haddad's Israeli-backed militia – plus the UN 'peacekeeping force'.

Israeli jets destroy an Iraqi nuclear plant near Baghdad.

1982
Argentine forces invade the Malvinas (Falkland Islands). Britain sends a piecemeal task force to resist. Nuclear submarine *Conqueror* sinks 47-year-old Argentine cruiser *General Belgrano* 56 km (38 miles) *outside* the 'Exclusion Zone' unilaterally declared by Tory Prime Minister Thatcher, desperate to improve lowest-ever approval ratings for any British prime minister. The Argentinian occupiers, almost all teenage conscripts, surrender to British marines and paratroopers. The Royal Navy loses two destroyers and two frigates to Exocet missiles.

1982 Israeli troops invade Lebanon, occupy Tyre and Sidon, then besiege West Beirut, a stronghold of the Palestine Liberation Organization (PLO).

1983 Ronald Reagan dubs the Soviet Union the 'Evil Empire' and announces the strategic defence initiative (aka 'Star Wars') which will provide the continental USA with a full shield against missile attack. Reagan also backs the Contra rebels who are engaged in terrorism against the Sandinista government of Nicaragua.

Civil war in Sri Lanka: the Sinhalese government in the south opposed by Tamil Tigers in the north of the island. The death toll is over 2,000.

Grenada's prime minister, Maurice Bishop, is killed in a palace coup. Reagan sends 6,000 troops to invade the island. They storm the beaches and *win*.

1984 Upper Volta is renamed 'Burkina Faso' ('the republic of honest men').

1985 French secret agents sink the Greenpeace flagship *Rainbow Warrior* in Auckland Harbour. Palestinians hijack the cruise liner *Achille Lauro* and kill a wheelchair-bound American-Jewish passenger. Israeli aircraft bomb Palestine Liberation Organization HQ in Tripoli and kill 60 people. The republic of honest men fights a border war with Mali.

1986 The Sithifran apartheid regime launches combined land and air raids against alleged ANC bases in three countries – Botswana, Zambia and Zimbabwe.

1987 Indian peacekeepers in Sri Lanka attempt to keep apart the Tamil Tigers and forces of the Colombo government.

1988 Laos versus Thailand border dispute involves fire fights for several weeks.

Soviet troops begin to evacuate Afghanistan after nine years' occupation.

USS *Vincennes* accidentally shoots down an Iranian airliner over international waters in the Persian Gulf, killing 290 people.

Ronald Reagan refuses a visa to Yasser Arafat to address the General Assembly in New York. The Assembly moves to Geneva to hear him.

1990
Iraq invades Kuwait. The USA recruits 33 nations as subservient partners and sends thousands of tanks to Saudi Arabia to threaten Saddam Hussein.

1991 'Operation Desert Storm' begins: The M1 Abrahams tank destroys the Republican Guard and the 'Mother of all Battles' is over in 100 hours.

Following their defeat in Afghanistan, the Union of Soviet Socialist Republics disintegrates – and so does Yugoslavia.

1992 UN peacekeepers in Somalia are in trouble – two American Black Hawk helicopters are brought down.

1993 Iraq is bombed regularly by the RAF and USAF, to enforce the 'no-fly' zones ordered in Iraqi airspace.

More US casualties in Somalia: 19 men die in the Battle of Mogadishu. Approval is finally given for combat roles for women in the US military.

1994 Bloody civil war in Rwanda. Up to 500,000 Tutsis are killed by Hutus. The huge 'coalition' force still in Saudi Arabia sits inert, as does the rest of the world. Though bombing raids do continue in Iraq.

1996 Another US military casualty-list of 19 dead men, this time in Saudi Arabia, when a marine barracks is destroyed by high explosive.

1997 Peruvian army commandos storm the Lima residence of the Japanese ambassador to end a 126-day hostage siege. A total of 14 Tupac Amaru rebel soldiers are killed.

In another insurgency, up to a thousand wilayans (villagers) are massacred by gunmen in the Relizane area of Algeria.

1998 India demonstrates its own nuclear bomb. There is a peace treaty, at last, in Northern Ireland.

US air strike on Al-Shifa, a pharmaceutical plant in Sudan, producing more than half of the country's medicines. The eventual death toll is estimated at 20,000, including at least 16,000 children who were dependent on the drugs produced at Al-Shifa. USA claims that the cruise missile strike was 'counter-terrorism', but the State Department later described it as 'an accident'.

1999 The North Atlantic Treaty Organization, the military alliance which lost its putative enemy as the Warsaw Pact drained away, finally goes into combat after 50 years. Apart from a brief action in 1995 against the elusive Republika Srpska, NATO had been shadow-boxing. Now its aircraft bomb the former Yugoslavia, to deter Serbian forces from attacking Croatia, and ground troops are committed to stop the vile and violent Serbian policy of 'ethnic cleansing', more accurately a type of mobile genocide.

“ I never read the proclamations of generals before battle, the speeches of fuhrers and prime ministers ... without seeming to hear in the background a chorus of raspberries from all the millions of common men to whom these high sentiments have no appeal. ”

George Orwell

2000 Israel celebrates the millennium – or Rosh Hashanah, 5760 – by withdrawing its troops from Lebanon after an occupation lasting 22 years, nearly half the history of the IDF's (Israel Defence Force's) existence.

North and South Korea sign a peace accord.

Kostunica replaces Slobodan Milosevic, the Butcher of Belgrade, Serbia's disgraced leader, after some violent clashes in the streets and violent explosions from the air.

2001 Milosevic is taken to the International Court at The Hague for trial as a war criminal.

The US submarine *Greeneville* surfaces directly under a Nipponese trawler and nine Honshu fishermen drown.

2001
On 11 September, nine Islamic extremists crash airliners into the World Trade Center in New York and into the Pentagon, in Washington. On 5 October the biggest bombing campaign since Vietnam begins, directed against the Taliban regime in Kabul, Afghanistan. The Taliban's authority collapses on 9 December after ground forces of the Northern Alliance chew up all the ammunition that the Taliban possess.

"To say it looks like a war zone and to tell you about bodies and blood in the street would not begin to describe what it's like. It's unimaginable, devastating, unspeakable carnage"

Firefighter Scott O'Grady of the Fire Department of New York, 11 September 2001

2002 Operation Anaconda: the Pentagon sends troops into Afghanistan to kill al-Qaida members. Two USAF F-16 aircraft bomb and kill four Canadian infantrymen, again dismissed as 'friendly fire'.

Bush addresses the UN, describing the 'grave and gathering danger' posed by the Iraqi regime.

2003 US Secretary of State Colin Powell presents evidence to the UN concerning the threat of Saddam Hussein's Weapons of Mass Destruction (WMD). A week later, more than 10 million people in 60 cities across the world protest against the haste to invade Iraq.

WMDS AND THE IRAQ WAR
2003

During his presidency, Saddam Hussein was internationally known for his use of chemical weapons against civilians in the Iran-Iraq war of the early 1980s. Following the 1991 Gulf War, he was involved in a long stand-off with the United Nations and international weapons inspectors, eventually culminating with the invasion of Iraq by American forces and 'the coalition of the willing' in 2003, when Saddam Hussein was overthrown, tried for war crimes and eventually executed.

Great controversy emerged when no stockpiled weapons of mass destruction were actually found, despite many American and British assertions that Saddam Hussein's regime posed an imminent threat to western security. This lead to widespread accusations that the American and British governments had inflated claims concerning Iraq's weapons capabilities, in order to pave the way for an invasion. Whilst some weapons of mass destruction, and weapon components from the 1980s and early 1990s, have been found, the general consensus is that the Iraqi regime did indeed cease stockpiling weapons in 1991. The US maintains that Hussein never abandoned his intentions to resume his chemical weapons program as soon as sanctions were lifted, and that something had to be done to stop him before it was too late.

On 20 March, American and British forces invade Iraq. By 3 April, US army painters and signwriters are changing the name of Saddam International Airport to 'Baghdad International Airport'.

On May Day, Bush lands on an aircraft carrier named after Abraham Lincoln, and declares 'Mission Accomplished'.

2004 Colin Powell resigns from his post and National Security Advisor, Condoleezza Rice becomes secretary of state. Hundreds of people are killed and injured by car bombs and suicide bombers around Baghdad and Fallujah, where a massive assault by US forces from 7 to 13 November, causing nearly 1,000 casualties, suggests that the 'Mission' is far from accomplished.

2005 Bombs kill hundreds more in Iraq, including Rafek Hariri, former prime minister of Lebanon, who is inside the heavily fortified, 'totally secure' Green Zone around American military HQ in central Baghdad. But the military–industrial complex continues to thrive, with the construction of the multi-billion-dollar Northrop Grumman X-47B, the world's first unmanned surveillance-and-attack aeroplane that can operate from both land bases and aircraft carriers.

2006 The US navy removes USS *Wisconsin* and USS *Iowa*, its remaining Iowa-class ships, from the Naval Vessel Register, ending a full century of the battleship.

The war with Iraq continues. Air strikes on Baqouba kill 80 people in order to assassinate Abu Musab al-Zarqawi, an al-Qaida leader who was on Saddam Hussein's death list for many years.

Israel takes revenge for the kidnap of three of its soldiers by bombing two-thirds of the Lebanon into rubble. The UN calls this 'disproportionate'.

An air strike on a madrasah in Bajaur, Afghanistan, kills dozens of suspected al-Qaida and Taliban militants.

The war in Somalia rumbles on, too. An African peacekeeping force, headed by Ethiopian troops, having destroyed most of the so-called 'warlords', take Mogadishu without a shot and establish some peace.

2007 An American AC-130 gunship is able to distinguish al-Qaida members of the Islamic Courts Union (ICU) in Somalia, entering a battle between the ICU and Ethiopian-supported government forces near Ras Kamboni. Most of the 60 people killed by the American intervention appear to be civilians, including several women and at least four children, but Pentagon briefers give assurances that they were all al-Qaidans.

Truck bombings in Baghdad markets kill 135 people and wound 339. A similar attack on the Bagram Air Base in Afghanistan kills 23. US Vice-President Cheney is visiting at the time, but is not injured. NATO troops, later branded 'incompetent' by US Defence Secretary Robert Gates, respond with dozens of assaults on Taliban positions in Helmand province.

The Iran revolutionary guard seizes 15 Royal Navy sailors and marines from HMS *Cornwall* in the Shatt-al-Arab waterway. The British Ministry of Defence presents maps to the world's media showing that their two-boat patrol was in Iraqi waters when challenged. The entire group is released after 10 days, and several of the hostages sell their stories to the British media. The British Army withdraws from the city of Basra in early September.

The newly elected Australian prime minister, Kevin Rudd, announces that all Australian military personnel will be withdrawn from Iraq by mid 2008.

2008 The Russian navy returns to the Bay of Biscay for the first time since the collapse of the Soviet Union.

The Israelis resume bombing the Gaza Strip in their most intense air strikes since 2005.

Fighting breaks out between Russia and The Democratic Republic of Georgia when Georgia launches a military strike against South Ossetia. In response the Russians send tanks in to Georgia. NATO demands that Russian troops pull out of Georgia immediately, so that Russia, Georgia and South Ossetia can begin peace talks. The USA and the UK demand a ceasefire and the ominous words 'Cold War' begin to be bandied about by politicians on both sides of the conflict.

“Only the dead have seen the end of war”

Plato

Picture Credits

The publisher would like to thank the following for permission to reproduce photographs:

Getty Images: 13 © National Geographic/Getty Images / **15**, **18**, **20**, **23**, **27**, **30**, **51**, **53**, **54**, **60**, **78**, **84**, **85**, **102**, **114**, **125**, **130**, **134**, **136**, **147**, **149**, **153**, **156** © Getty Images / **19**, **24**, **29**, **57**, **62**, **92**, **137**, **146**, **148**, **154** © Time & Life Pictures/Getty Images / **22**, **36**, **38** © Roman/The Bridgeman Art Library/Getty Images / **46** © French School/Getty Images / **52**, **68**, **87**, **118**, **126**, **127**, **140** © Popperfoto/Getty Images / **58** © Tsuneo Yamashita/Getty Images / **61** © Hisham Ibrahim/Getty Images / **65** © Ira Block/Getty Images / **72**© The Palma Collection/Getty Images / **83** © English School/Getty Images / **80** © Victor Mikhailovich Vasnetsov/The Bridgeman Art Library/Getty Images / **96** © English School/Getty Images / **103**, **131** © Roger Viollet/Getty Images / **104** © Baron Louis Albert Bacler d'Albe/The Bridgeman Art Library/Getty Images / **122** © Charles Edwin Fripp/The Bridgeman Art Library/Getty Images / **150**, **152**, **157** © AFP/Getty Images.

Corbis Images: 11 © Walter Bibikow/JAI/Corbis / **31**, **79**, **81**, **95**, **113**, **132**, **133** © Bettmann/CORBIS / **37** © Araldo de Luca/CORBIS / **40** © Vanni Archive/CORBIS / **77** © Stapleton Collection/Corbis / **107** © Historical Picture Archive/CORBIS / **124**, **144** © CORBIS / **128** © Hulton-Deutsch Collection/CORBIS / **135** © Burstein Collection/CORBIS.

Bridgeman Images: 32 © Louvre, Paris, France/The Bridgeman Art Library / **48** © Prado, Madrid, Spain/The Bridgeman Art Library / **56** © Private Collection, The Stapleton Collection/The Bridgeman Art Library / **69** © Louvre, Paris, France, Lauros/Giraudon/The Bridgeman Art Library / **71**, **99** © Look and Learn/The Bridgeman Art Library / **86** © Boston Public Library, Boston, Massachusetts, USA/The Bridgeman Art Library / **93**, **106** © Musee de la Marine, Paris, France, J.P. Zenobel/The Bridgeman Art Library / **94**, **97** © Private Collection, Ken Welsh/The Bridgeman Art Library / **98**, **101**, **109**, **121** © Private Collection/The Bridgeman Art Library / **100** © Gerald Coke Handel Collection, Foundling Museum, London/The Bridgeman Art Library / **105** © Chateau de Versailles, France/The Bridgeman Art Library / **108** © Private Collection, Peter Newark American Pictures/The Bridgeman Art Library / **110** © Musee des Beaux-Arts, Lille, France, Lauros/Giraudon/The Bridgeman Art Library / **112** © Library of Congress, Washington D.C., USA/The Bridgeman Art Library / **120** © Bibliotheque Nationale, Paris, France/The Bridgeman Art Library / **123** © Leeds Museums and Galleries (City Art Gallery) U.K./The Bridgeman Art Library.